Sip & Savor

Edmond Bruneau

ISBN: 978-1-936769-10-0
Library of Congress Control Number: 2023943069

Cover Design: Edmond Bruneau and Donna Lange
Editor: Donna Lange

Previous books by Edmond Bruneau
Prescription for Advertising - 1986
Colors of My Within - 2011
New Hues and Past Tales - 2016
The Totem - 2018
Walla Walla Sweet - 2021

Lyricist for:
Robot Raven's Greatest Hits - Part One - 2015
Robot Raven's Greatest Hits - Part Two - 2016
Life Goes On by Robot Raven - 2017
Set to Soar by Robot Raven - 2018
Robot Raven Rockers - 2018
Kick Back Relax by Robot Raven - 2020
Sunflower 69 by Whistlewit - 2022
Country Cousins by The Cow Cats - 2023

For my grandchildren,
Natalie and Garrett.

May you never loose
your imagination or
wonderment of life.

FORWARD

Like a fine wine, poetry should be sipped,
savored and enjoyed. 150 new poems in this book
await your pleasure to read and treasure.
Written while living in Walla Walla, where wine
tasting is a common activity, the idea for a
"poem tasting" came to me, since a single poem
can be imbibed, swirled around in your mind,
leaving notes of delight and enlightenment.
You'll find the original poems in this book to be
a nice variety of flavors – some thoughtful, some
amusing, some forthright, some plainspoken.
Just like a wine tasting, you'll discover ones that
are your favorites and others you might pour back
in the dump bucket. The challenge, of course, is
to find the poems that have meaning for you and
allow them to become a part of you in the process.
Fortunately, you don't have to select just one bottle
to take home. All the varietals are right here in this
book, ready for your exploration, discovery and
evaluation during your next poem tasting.

If you find you enjoy the samplings and want to
explore further, let me suggest some library
poems from my four previous books of poetry.
They've been kept cool and aged nicely.
It's my hope that some of my poems become your
poems, too. It's the greatest compliment a writer
can acheive.

Edmond Bruneau

TABLE OF CONTENTS

Empty Book

Empty book, naked.
No letters to clothe.
No calories, nourishment.
Nothing for a mind to hold.

Blank pages, hollow promise.
One so much like the other.
Vacancy blinks neon –
lures in tales to be told.

Empty book sits, waits
for someone to write it.
Fill pages with poetry,
stories, thoughts, emotions.

Writer writes to reader unknown.
Prays content appreciated.
Valued. Cherished. Admired.
Thankful for being chosen.

Filling up an empty book –
the risk writers take to share.
Releasing their inner self –
soul laid out bare.

Empty book, always desolate
until inhabited with words.
Then its heart begins beating.
Life on its own, somewhere.

Curse the Cursor

Cursor is blinking,
demanding to be fed
words, thoughts, ideas.
Blank screen impatiently
awaits a beginning.
Starving for content.
Nagging for nourishment.

My responsibility –
to satisfy its insistence
and fulfill its hunger.
Writer's block,
with me in its grips,
frozen to supply content.
Unable to access muse.

Blank screen so lonely
without black letters
that give purpose to
its existence. It pleads
to a painter without paints –
writer without words –
who fears the commanding cursor.

Inspiration may just be shy,
waiting for the right time
to make her grand entrance.
A waiting game writers play
while she primps and preens
prior to eventual emergence –
satisfying cursor's appetite.

Heart and Mind

I am man
of heart and mind.
Time – friend and enemy.
The ultimate irony.

Children grown, on their own,
still call me Dad on Christmas.
Relieved of responsibility.
New identity – whimsical remedy.

No longer hides
from former self.
Effort to improve diminishing health –
keep the bear at bay.

Heart merged second time around.
Love develops, expands,
sturdy in our hands –
passionately profound.

Mind, more than mush –
maybe not as robust,
deft or dexterous
as it was in its prime.

Yet, there's still time
to create poems with reason,
perhaps with rhyme.
Songs still to be sung as they align to shine.

I am muddled together,
with cable, cords and twine
and continue to be the man I am –
enduring heart and mind.

Real Boy

My façade –
flesh not fir.
Soul more
than skin deep.

Inner heart
pump station
palpitates
my plasma.

I'm not wooden.
Or fit into a
chiseled image
created by another.

My being
grows, changes,
improves, ages,
inside and out.

I need no
manipulator or
ventriloquist to
speak my truth.

No one
pulls my strings
or puts words
in my mouth.

I am unique.
One of a kind.
Most important –
a real boy.

Open Sésame

Magic words
open the door
with ease,
unlocking reward
of genuine gems.

No gold
in this treasure.
Instead, an
abundance of faith,
balance and harmony.

Further search reveals
more impressive trove.
Finespun forgiveness.
Doubloons of delight.
Silk of self-motivation.

Jewels of Joy.
Pearls of perception.
Cache of choice.
Horde of honesty.
Incandescent intuition.

Such richness
overlooked by
those not worthy.
Discovery – a
rare profit, indeed.

What could contain
anything more precious?
It's there for you
for the taking
with your affirmation.

Imaginary Friend

Like a shadow, you were always there,
deciding the direction, especially
when we came to a fork in the road.

You knew just when
to rest and relax.
I'd count on you for that.

Valuable companion.
Lent an ear to my fears.
Steered me from wrong to right.

Didn't have to earn your trust.
You were with me. Everyday.
Ready, willing and able.

Your friendship had
a profound effect.
Love without conditions.

In many ways your presence
made me more complete.
Sidekick with bright spirit.

I see you in the mirror and
think how remarkable it is
that you look so similar to me.

We could have been brothers.
Even twins. Not hard to imagine.
But, I like you just the way you are.

Before, No More

Before they arrived,
nature
was our mother.
Went where
the bounty was –
thrived off game,
roots and herbs.
Moved with seasons.
Slept with dreams.

Traded
within our tribe
and with other clans.
Things of value.
No word for money.
No coins.
No gold or silver.
Peace pipes. Powwows.
Singing the wise old songs.

Centuries upon centuries,
we lived this way until
the strangers came.
Killed our game.
Made agreements
with shiny trinkets.
Treated our mother
with disrespect.
Changed our world.

Some
accepted new brothers
so we could live in peace.
Others wanted old ways.
Moved further away until
there was no place left.
Gone, the same earth
where ancestors prospered.
Before, no more.
Before, no more.
Before, no more.

Kitten

Even though she is five years old,
Donna still calls her Kitten.
Something attacked her this week –
probably a hawk or a turkey.

Tami had prominent claw lacerations.
Multiple puncture wounds. Sutures required.
Vet shaved fur in multiple places
so we could monitor her wounds.

She's healing. Getting better.
Last night, the snugglepuss
laid next to me while watching TV.
Kitten whiskers tickled my leg.

Maybe it's time to rethink
whether our indoor/outdoor cats
should be indoor/kennel cats instead.
Vet bills would certainly be lower.

Besides the requisite mouse or mole,
she's also brought us a baby turtle,
a slithering snake and a lazy lizard.
Adventures that may now be memories.

Selfishly, we'd like her to stick around.
Depriving her from free range –
trade for a longer, safer life.
For both the cats – and our sanity.

Shadow of Himself

All I can see now
is your shadow.
Parroting what
it believes was you.
Three dimensional you,
gone from view –
shady self, emerged.

I remember when your
shadow was secondary,
mimicking every move.
Growing taller as
the sun journeyed
toward the horizon,
stretching your importance.

Cloudy days,
it disappeared.
Leaving you alone
to deal with
the real world
without its support
and sleight of hand.

Truth illuminates
your devoted shadow
distinctly –
and you, less visible –
hiding behind it,
fearing recognition
and responsibility.

I see you no longer.
Your shallow
one dimensional shadow puppet
remains casting images
against the wall,
disregarding depth or detail.
Shadows have no soul.

Young McEvil

McEvil Clown

Greasepaint
transformed
personality.
Escape
from reality.
Transfigure.
Alter ego.
Jester. Mime.
Balloon animals
intertwined.
Innocence.
Painted smile
Kind heart.
Sweet grin.
Played the part.
Passage of time.
Boy clown
to manhood.
No longer
understood.
Cute cast aside.
Lot more scary.
Aspect of age.
Burdened brain.
Turn of page.
Good to evil.
Malevolent intent.
Wolf in clown clothing.
Hidden frown.
Full of self loathing.
Invades
nightmares
for amusement.
Creepy. Chilling.
Malicious malcontent.
Paint on
friendly smirk.
Halloween.
And everyday
in between.

Old McEvil

The Cubs Game

Dear Don,
One of the unwritten benefits of printing in Chicago
was going to a Cubs game with you. Even when
you sold the company, it was always arranged
for me to sit with you in your box seats –
a few rows up from home plate. *What a perspective!*
I remember walking to the game from your
21st floor condo on West Diversey. We'd stroll past
the neighborhood where you grew up. You would
elaborate what it was like to live in a greystone
and expound about the characters residing there,
including Tom Bosley, your cousin.
For you, those truly were your *"Happy Days."*
I'd get the peanuts and we'd find a hot dog stand
before getting to Wrigley Field. You always
made sure I had a couple beers during the game.
Always felt like an honored guest.
I remember a young lady in front of our seats
eating peanuts, shell and all, without a second thought.
Seeing Darius Rucker a few boxes down watching the game.
Singing *"Take Me Out to the Ballgame"* with Harry Caray
during the seventh inning stretch.
Pitching sensation Kerry Wood hit a homer for us
past the ivy-laden green wall. Whether the Cubs
won or lost, it was always an honor to sit in a stadium
where Babe Ruth, Lou Gehirg, Ty Cobb, Ted Williams
and Hank Aaron played as the visiting team.
After the game, we'd take a jaunt through
Wrigleyville before heading home. You told me
you were impressed with the gay community
cleaning up what used to be a seedy area.
Last Christmas, you called and told me you had cancer.
Bottom of the ninth. Praying for extra innings.
For me, you always hit it out of the park.
Go Cubs.

Aneurysm

36 years old, she was
ready to begin another
Little League season.
A graduate from
Lake Washington High School
two years after Dad.
Both were Kangaroos.

Connie helped support the
baseball club for 14 years,
starting at the concession stand –
ending as treasurer.
My father – new president
of the organization –
sought her guidance.

Rainy May Saturday.
Hopped into our light tan
'66 Plymouth Belvedere
with Dad to run errands.
Last stop was Connie's.
"Stay in the car," he said.
No radio. Staccato raindrops.

Confined in beige interior,
believing it would be
a few minutes like
the rest of the errands.
I was wrong. Patiently and
impatiently imprisoned
for an hour and a half.

Connie was a charmer
with looks to match.
Dad wasn't a cheater,
but he was a flirt.
However important the
discussion must have been,
I felt forgotten, abandoned.

He must have had
a cup of coffee, or two.
Let the enchanting lady
help him lose track of time.
Cadence of the wipers –
percussion to my whining
on our way home.

Two weeks later,
Connie died.
Sudden brain aneurysm.
Shocked community.
Front page news in
the local newspaper.
Funeral service 6/10/68.

The flag, half-mast
the whole season
at Buckley Field.
Concession stand
renamed in her honor.
Never ordered a
"graveyard" snowcone again.

I now wonder what
took place in those
notorious 90 minutes.
Likely innocent.
If it was an affair,
the aneurysm
put an end to it.

Two of a Cline

Him hardware, her software.
Together became harmony.
Symbiotic shadows in
tangent tango tripping
the light fantastic as
both souls danced.

Him left, her right.
Sweet and savory.
Pen and paper.
Soap and water.
Salt and pepper.
Bacon and eggs.

Him wine, her cheese.
Apples and oranges –
same fruit basket.
Two sides of coin
sharing same value.
Stabilized seesaw.

Him fire, her water.
Limbo between
heaven and hell.
Baked Alaska.
Flaming cherries jubilee.
Flint and steel sparks.

Him yin, her yang.
Black and white.
Painting grey together.
Discovering color
from each other's pallet.
Art that's theirs alone.

Caught Smiling

He was caught smiling at her.
Wasn't a secret, really.
She knew without a doubt.
Delighted. Tickled her heart.
Today was the day
he broke his silence
inspired by her smile back.
Today was the day
he would be brave.
Appearing calm as he could be
even though inside he felt
his heart might explode
at any minute.
Juggernaut could not be stopped.
The magical moment
when he said
"How do you do?"
And ever so grateful when she replied,
"Quite well, thank you. You?"
For him, it was a miracle.
Unbelievable.
Bashful days and lonely nights
vanished from his mind.
New freedom. New honesty.
He replied earnestly,
"Best I've ever been, I believe."
It gave her another smile.
So sincere. So corny.
She knew he was the one.

Relentless

If I decide to love you,
prepare for full throttle.
I don't know how to
drive slowly in school zones or
brake suddenly at intersections.

My love is constant –
no matter the hill or valley,
I am steadfast
in depth of frigid winter
or sweltering summer sun.

The ride we take together –
straightaways and curves.
We may see paths differently
nor do everything the same –
love's rock-solid, regardless.

If you decide to love me,
you'll be able to help
take my foot off the gas
and relax into the
destination we call life.

Be gentle with my heart.
It's large enough to
allow another in –
vulnerable enough to
bleed when bruised.

My love surrounds, not smothers –
like a warm tropical breeze with
fragrance of reassurance
mildly blowing through your hair.
You'll always know it's there.

Hook or by Crook

My love, resolute.
Purposeful. Steadfast.
Unwavering. Absolute.
Constant. Earnest. Vast.

Embedded in my DNA.
The whole of me
knows no other way –
until we become we.

Force of nature.
Relentless. Dead set.
Easy money wager.
Better than a good bet.

Bound and determined.
Staunch. Tenacious.
Persistent. Genuine.
Loyal. Gracious.

No stone unturned.
Nothing overlooked.
Stern to stern.
Hook or by crook.

What is Love?

Love – a flower.
Gentle beauty as it buds.
Then blossoms –
Petals emerge.
Resonate allure.
Sweet smell of efflorescence.
You want to
cut the stem.
Put in a vase.
Display on the table
for all to appreciate.
But then, blooms fade.

Nurture the whole of it,
roots and all.
Keep it viable with care.
The plant becomes
larger, stronger,
even more beautiful
than before.
Smiles in sunlight.
Romance in rain.
Matures and thrives.
Flourishes, even in
stormy weather.

Begins with a flower –
grows into a garden.
Till rich soil for
necessary nutrients.
Never neglect
this precious,
extraordinary gift.
Keep love vital
and alive.
Let it multiply
beyond all
expectations.

Conquer with Kindness

When
peace lacks promise.
Benevolence looks bleak.
Competition for conversation
not the resolve we seek.

When
sharp tongues slash sympathy.
Grimace absent of grace.
Remarks without retreat.
Words won't get erased.

There is
a way to smooth it out.
Way for blaze to breathe.
Replace clash with kindness.
Let resentment leave.

There are
blankets for the blizzard.
Better possibilities envisioned.
Compassion for adversity –
healing the division.

Kindness is
the sword of choice
with shield for protection.
No matter what the battle,
love is the deflection

Love, not time, heals all wounds.
– Andy Rooney

Love, the Magic Potion

Love, the magic potion.
Rejuvenate. Repair.
Relieve. Renew.
All things troubling you.

Cure for heartbreak.
Emotional laceration.
Trauma. Distress.
Applies a warm compress.

Love, the salve.
Balm. Cream.
Liniment. Lotion.
Compassionate devotion.

Perfect prescription –
Sympathy. Sensitivity
Empathy. Tenderness.
Cure-all, more than less.

It's love, not time
that truly mends.
Panacea for every ill.
Better than any pill.

Contemplation

In this life, we are given time
and decide on how to spend it.
If fortunate enough to be given love
it matters how we tend it.

Man seeks life's meaning.
Longs for eyes to see it.
The quest is to find your truth.
Have courage then to be it.

Light of day, dark of night –
better than if we dreamt it.
World of reality. The end depends
on just how long you rent it.

Buyer's Remorse

Save now.
Limited opportunity
because it's almost free!
Backed up
with proven results
and lifetime guarantee.

Promise of health,
love and safety.
Amazing new discovery.
Too good to be true –
Easy way
to part you from your money.

Gratitudes

Grateful for
morning wake –
Made it to another day.

Grateful for
looking over and seeing
my loving partner.

Grateful for
breakfast conversation
and pickleball.

Grateful for
Daughter, Son-in-law,
and two grandkids.

Grateful for
Son, Daughter-in-law –
wine tasting whim.

Grateful for
blessing of friends –
some old, some new.

Grateful for
writing with
heart and soul.

Grateful for
playfulness, imagination
and creativity.

Grateful for
laughter. Tears.
Life worth living.

Grateful for
two black and white
crazy cow cats.

Grateful for
nature and all
its majesty.

Grateful for
sight. Sound.
Taste. Touch. Smell.

Grateful for
music. Dance.
Entertainment.

Grateful for
ordinary days
and adventures.

Grateful for
compassion and
understanding.

Grateful for
food in my stomach.
Clothes on my back.

Grateful for
roof over my head.
Nurturing community.

Grateful for
peace with my
mortal spirituality.

Grateful for
sleep transporting
me to tomorrow.

Needle and Thread

Tear
in need
of stitches.
Hole
requires
repair.
Mended
with
needle
and thread –
skill
and patience –
provision
and practicality.

Patched.
Fixed.
Broken wing
flies again
once more.
Repaired.
Restored.
Rejuvenated.
Needle
and thread.
Heart unsaid.
Sewn together
by fingers
of love.

Klepto Kissmet

Acquired my attraction.
Appeased my amour.
Embezzled my embrace.
Ripped off our rapport.

Looted my love.
Ignited my infatuation.
Facilitated my fondness.
Derailed our devotion.

Stole my sentiment.
Robbed my romance.
Kidnapped my kindness.
Dispatched our dance.

Fanned my flame.
Heisted my heart
Poached my passion.
Swindled from the start.

Klepto Kissmet.
Took all my trust.
Abducted my affection.
Larcenous lust.

Sisters

Remember when?
Made sandcastles
with tin buckets
and plastic shovels.

Many trips
from the seashore
gathering water
for the moat.

Me, Lady Elizabeth.
You, Countess Christina.
Each waiting for
Prince Charming to arrive.

We would imagine
our lives older.
Next door neighbors.
Offspring playing as cousins.

You escaped the castle
at seventeen,
with a Marine, no less.
Me, year behind, alone.

You lived far away.
I stayed at home until
the handsome harbormaster
moored this maiden's heart.

Life didn't turn out
as we imagined.
Still sisters. Still connected.
Close as letter or phone call.

Women do outlive their men.
Time to be together again.
Helping grandkids build
their own castle dreams.

Wonderful to sit –
each wearing sandals
on an old painted bench
in the Florida ocean sun.

Talk more than walk.
Share stories of our lives.
Savoring sand and surf.
Akin, like old times.

"Life shrinks or expands in proportion to one's courage."
– Anaïs Nin

Lion Heart

You were brave –

greeting an
unknown world,
newly born.

stepping up to
the school bus and
watching mom wave good-bye.

receiving bad marks
for coloring
outside the lines.

being sick at home,
alone, watching
the assassination.

learning to swim
in the cold water
of Gateway Grove.

asking for a dance
even though the
answer was *"No."*

having strength to endure
tooth straightening
for four long years.

bearing the
humiliation of failing
your first Driver's Test.

getting married
at the ripe age
of twenty-one.

starting your
own business
from the ground up.

supporting two kids,
conception
through college.

being the caregiver,
watching cancer
negate your nuptials.

dealing with
your own disease
and disorders.

risking an
open heart
to find love again.

surviving the stress of
building a new home
in a new town.

You are brave.
You are courage.
You are lion heart.

From the Heart

I want to stay around awhile,
though I know I've let you down
at least a couple of times.

You're exercising frequently. Thanks.
Wish you had done it sooner,
but better late than never.

I have a stent in me
from your heart attack in 2011.
Really messed up Christmas.

My flutter and atrial fibrillation
put you into a 7-day ICU ten years later.
A double ablation steadied my rhythm.

You're eating smaller meal portions
and I'm proud of you.
I love the fruits and grains for breakfast.

You always eat your vegetables.
Even the occasionally served kale.
Whole wheat. High fiber. No doughnuts.

I don't expect you to be perfect.
You eat eggs, fish, low-fat dairy and lean meats.
And only bacon, brats, butter once in a while.

Your sodium intake is commendable.
I wish I could wean you off tomato juice,
but without salt it's terrible.

Besides the damage disease has already done,
I'm hoping you live through your seventies.
Maybe into your eighties with some luck.

Everyone needs an indulgence now and then.
Some chips won't derail your good intentions.
Carrots and celery are better, however.

I love you and want to continue beating as long
as humanly possible. Do both of us a favor.
Just think of me a little more often, please.

Faint of Heart

There are those who rise up –
ascend the difficult climb.
Determination. Tenacity.
The lion-hearted kind.

Face adversity straight on.
There for others' needs.
When the going gets tough
they go forward, not recede.

Then, there's faint of heart –
exact opposite of valor.
Shy away from suffering –
such silence can't be louder.

Squeamish. Frightened.
Unable to offer support.
No backbone for crisis.
Completely out-of-sorts.

Ordeals simply continue
while emotionally fatigued.
Polite phrase for cowardice –
faint of heart, indeed.

From frying pan to fire.
Dealing with the unexpected.
Facing those tough times
when one's resolve is tested.

Time for courage. Bravery.
Choice of meek or bold.
True self – naked, revealed.
Steadfast or simply fold?

Test of heartfelt humanness –
the answer, yes or no.
Moment of truth, a turning point –
which way to choose to go.

Valentine Hearts

SMITTEN, MY KITTEN

I'LL BE YOUR CANDY DANDY

AFFECTION CONFECTION

INFATUATION REVELATION

ASPIRED DESIRE

FLIRT ALERT

JUBILANT LUBRICANT

DNA BOUQUET

UNCHASTE EMBRACE

KISS OF BLISS

RATION OF PASSION

TENDERNESS EXPRESS

NAUGHTY HOTTIE

GEORGY PORGY ORGY

MOONSTRUCK SCHMUCK

DON'T BOGART MY HEART

GIVE LOVE A SHOVE

BURNING YEARNING

WOO OVERDUE

Mixed Media

Adjust easel.
Gesso canvas.
Keep your concept clean.
You are the painter
of your point of view.
One who sees the scene.

Blend colors
Create shades.
Pigments to your palette.
Brush you choose
determines the stroke.
Only because you allow it.

Maybe it's a mural.
Collage with collaboration.
Simple silhouette.
Every day –
new work of art,
revealing your reset.

Anew every sunrise.
On authority
of your own.
Pastels of possibilities.
Virtuoso vision –
yours, alone.

Lost time is never found again.
– Benjamin Franklin - ***Poor Richard's Almanac***

Lost Time

Time marches on.
Leaving behind
what could have been –
including past regrets.

Move forward.
All time allows.
Yesterday in the rear view.
No real reenactment.

Life bygone.
No going back.
Attempt to repair
steals time from today.

Time squandered. Finite.
Precious ticking clock
marking moments ahead –
sixty clicks a minute.

Why lament lost time?
Make it a sextant
not an anchor.
You may lose less of it.

Another $20 Donation

I know better.
Playing Powerball
for the $635 million prize.
Chances are infinitesimal.
Voluntary tax.

Feed the machine cash,
click a button,
shoot for the moon.
Spin the
wheel of fortune.

But what if...
What if I got lucky?
Instant millionaire.
Verified before
I get too excited.

The discussion begins.
What would I do
with all that dough?
Hatch a plan to help?
Give it all away gratis?

Precarious position.
Steer clear of crooks.
Maintain some decorum.
Be courageous or meek?
Industrious or lazy?

Would friends still be true
or like me for my money?
Winning the lottery would
make me suspicious. Leery.
Life a little less magical.

Tomorrow will come
and *"Not a Winner"*
unfortunately revealed.
Dreams can be nightmares.
Actually, I'm relieved.

I went to the animal fair,
The birds and the beasts were there,
The big baboon by the light of the moon
Was combing his auburn hair.
The monkey bumped the skunk,
And sat on the elephant's trunk;
The elephant sneezed and fell on his knees,
And that was the end of the monk!

  – from Animal Fair, traditional children's folk song.

Monkey Business

Take some tea with me.
Cappuccino if you prefer.
Let's enjoy the morning –
begin the day heartwarming.

Dad's nose behind the
black, white and read all over.
Worrying about yesterday,
but seemed so far away.

Newspaper's gone,
but now there's the phone.
Multi-tasking breakfast
while the other feels alone.

Looking into your eyes
while we sip our sunrise.
Sharing togetherness
without distractions or distress.

There will always be
an animal fair.
Birds and beasts
will ever be there.

Let's take this time
to forget our fears.
Learn about the monkey later –
realize these moments greater.

Our universe is full of
tragedies and turmoil.
Let's spend the morning together.
News robs us of our pleasure.

Plenty of time later
to absorb baboon beauty tips –
when an elephant simply slips
causing a monkey's life eclipse.

Take some tea with me.
Cappuccino if you prefer.
Enjoy our precious moments
before those negative components.

Barbed Wire

I remember when Grandpa
rebuilt the fence surrounding
our forty-five acre farm.
Ten-foot creosote poles,
eight inches in diameter
set four feet into the ground,
strung with five strands of barbed wire.
Built strong, like a fortress.

Fence corners featured
diagonal cross pieces
for even more
sturdiness and support.
Perfect way for a six-year old boy
to carefully climb the fence
and see surroundings
from a whole new height.

Carefully put hands
in between barbs.
Take it slow. Climb
the diagonal timber,
changing hand positions
onto the next higher strand
until the top is reached.
Descend the exact same way.

Did it a dozen times
without incident. Fun.
Playing with my
four-year old sister,
I brashly boasted
about my achievement.
Challenged her to
experience the same thrill.

Correctly showed how
it was done. Went first.
Gave a full demonstration.
She eagerly gave it a try.
Made it to the fourth strand
before she slipped –
a bleeding tear
across her right palm.

Ran to the house –
fetched a warm wet washcloth,
and wrapped it tightly around
her small gory red hand.
A call to the closest doctor
and we were in the car –
me assigned to keeping
the wrap tight while mom drove.

Ten stitches. Left a scar.
Remorse for the next decade.
A regret one can't recant.
The incident wasn't on purpose.
Being older, I was responsible
for her in my care.
A scar on my conscience
that may never fully heal.

I think about the ordeal
we experienced that day.
Shock, dismay and worry
my mother must have felt.
An unexpected expense
on an already tight budget.
A son she could no longer trust
with her daughter's safety.

The actual barbed wire fence of my youth.

What is Reality, Really?

Today's news
written from someone's perspective.
Yet, it becomes part of our reality
when taken at face value.
A mental reflex – as we must
base our own reality on something
besides personal experience.

Dreams are our own dreams.
Not someone else's.
The unconscious mind constantly
interpreting the pros and cons
of truth and falsehood.
Emerging with personal version
of what is real.

A question then remains,
when one loses touch with reality –
which reality are we referring?
The lost mind's reality is still real.
What yardstick, what methodology
chooses the correct reality
for the dark diagnosis?

Society's reality is certainly
not a coordinated consensus.
Politics, religion, economy, education
are paradoxical pieces of truth.
Perhaps a psychological analysis
can determine someone's inner nature.
What if the scientific method is flawed?

Reality is the dimension in which
we see through our lens –
focusing on expectations and values.
Yesterday's reality is far different than today's.
Constantly moving, modifying, mutating.
Personal journey that cannot be defined.
Reality like no other.

Wheels of Industry

Wheels turn.
Even when
hardware becomes soft
and software becomes hard.

Industrial revolution
still raging
without any sign
of machine malfunction.

Call it progress.
Essential to our lives.
Photo without film.
Phone with flashlight.

Wheels never stop
providing solutions
for problems
we never knew existed.

If not turning
at a power plant,
new ideas whirling
in mortal minds.

At its mercy
without escape.
As our lives revolve,
pivot and pirouette.

Young for My Age

Five-year-old birthday
days before Kindergarten began.
I remember the interview
with the Primary School principal –
make sure I was mature enough.
I made him laugh.

Up for the challenge. Eager. Excited.
Finally – to go to school
with nearly all classmates older.
Never thought being
young for my age
hindrance or handicap.

But if my parents had waited
until I was six?
I would have been
one of the older kids.
Advantage of another year.
Mental, physical and emotional growth.

Would it have changed my life?
Would I be a smarter student?
More confident? Assured?
Would I have been more ready
for social situations in
Junior High and High School?

If I could go back in time and
enter school at six instead of five –
which me would I like better?
Stronger for sports.
Different friends.
Come of age sooner.

Tempting as it might be
to imagine the difference
one year can make –
my struggles, my strife,
my ability to overcome odds
make up the whole of me.

The person I became because
I was young for my age.
Lessons learned along the way.
Accomplishments. Failures.
Contribution to my foundation –
framing my existence.

Not being a year behind,
but a year ahead, instead.
I am thankful my parents
thought I could handle school
early instead of late. Besides –
it got me out of the house.

Stuck in Traffic

Can't go forward,
can't go back.
Stuck in traffic with
the rest of the pack.
Progress only in
inches, not miles.
Transportation comrades
sport frowns, not smiles.
Two hours to destination,
two hours to return.
Eighth of a day
gone, wasted, burned.
Thousand hours a year
completely down the drain.
Reason for road rage
that drives drivers insane.
This is NOT
the American dream –
unfettered travel,
commuting, serene.
No, it's a corral of cattle
herded to slaughter.
Unable to escape the fate,
run instead of saunter.

You can cure this cancer,
if only you are willing.
Give up metropolitan ways –
find someplace else fulfilling.
There are still places
traffic jams don't exist.
Ten minutes to anywhere
without worry or risk.
Abandon the hamster wheel.
Take nature walks instead.
Gain those four hours back
and live before you're dead.

Sleuth

Determined to solve crime.
Tenacious in resolve.
Ingenuity; integrity.
Empowerment enthralled.

Competent instincts.
Caper clues confound.
Presence of a menace.
Depravity depth profound.

Criminal grounded.
Culprit and gun.
A thanks for the efforts.
Healing begun.

A sleuth is a blessing
detecting the uncouth.
Lives climb forward
dedicated to the truth.

Oasis

Bar in the middle of nowhere.
Promise of dancing in neon.
Beer on tap. Casino in back.
Live bait for sale, inside.

Squeezed between the
lumber yard and general store.
Dirt road out front –
oiled to keep dust down.

Aptly named, it is an oasis
in the quiet desolation
of a one-horse town
imitating civilization.

A place to escape
from
summer's inferno
and winter's bitter cold.

At night, street lights
illuminate the sidewalk
welcoming strangers
and patrons alike.

Cold beer and clientele
commiserate together
in dim incandescent light –
country on the jukebox.

Not a joint for lightweights.
This a place to get drunk.
Forget about troubles.
Numb nightmares, temporarily.

When the train stops,
passengers peer out
the window to see the Oasis
in its daylight disguise.

They don't see the Oasis
in its evening gown
magically turning sows' ears
into swanky silk purses.

To them, it's just an
annoying pause at the depot.
A place with no paved roads.
Where happy hours are never happy.

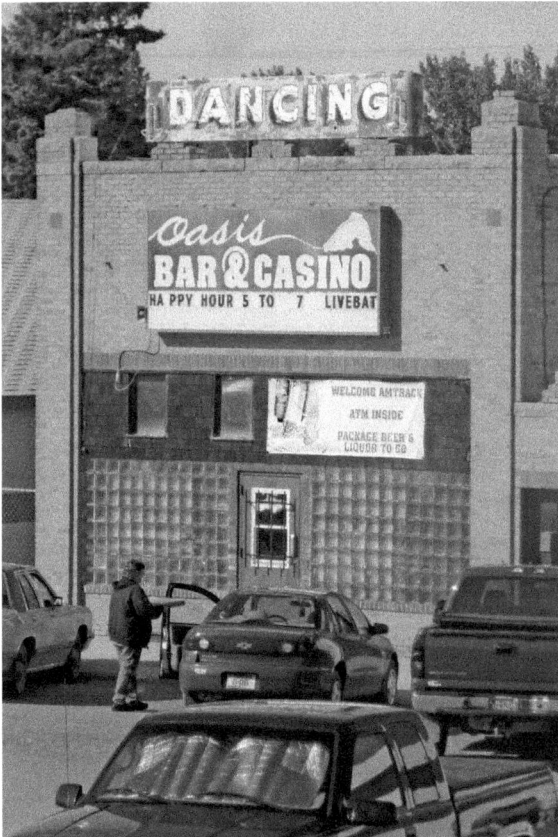

Suspension of Disbelief

Cast away
critical thinking.
Leave logic
at the door.
Imagine
the impossible.
Drink the Kool-Aid
as it's poured.

It's the key
to visit Tinseltown
where everything's
in disguise.
Illusion –
the delusion.
The remainder,
romanticized.

Like sausage –
you don't
want to know
how it's really made.
Just digest the
entertainment.
Give actors
their accolade.

See them
as they are –
cinematic artists
of their craft.
Playing characters
in a story to
make you cry
or laugh.

They do not
walk on water.
They are not
kings or queens.
They don't belong
on a pedestal
because of the
silver screen.

Suspend your belief,
revel in requiem
while you
enjoy the show.
Afterwards,
back to reality –
be ready to
say "hello."

Everest

Less than a year after
Jim Whittaker became
the first American to
conquer the formidably
perilous Mt. Everest,
I was presented with
my Cub of the Year prize
by Jim himself.

A celebrity
Redmond, Washington
claimed as its own.
His return from such
a remarkable achievement
was marked with a parade
and a packed house at
the Mond Theatre –
a proud town
welcoming their hero home.

The award took me
completely by surprise.
Flabbergasted!
Jim Whittaker was
shaking MY hand.
Congratulating ME.
Handing me a
huge sleeping bag
my ten-year old arms
could barely hold.

Jim may have climbed Everest,
but at that amazing moment
it was me who was
on top of the world.
Chances are,
I took longer to descend
from that summit
than him the actual one.

Whittaker once said,
*"You don't really
conquer a mountain.
You conquer yourself."*
One wonders what
life events help shape the
human being you become.
This was one of them.

*climb highest mountains,
transverse difficult valleys,
because they are there.*

CUB OF THE YEAR TALKS TO MAN OF THE YEAR — Eddie Bruneau, Cub Scout of Den 9, was presented the Cub of the Year award last Friday night at the annual Cub Scout Father-Son Banquet. Eddie is talking with Jim Whittaker, first American to reach the top of Mt. Everest, who recently received a Man of the Year Award. James Erickson, Cub of the Month, is at the right. Pierre Bruneau, Eddie's proud father, is at the left.

Eddie Bruneau is local Cub of the Year

Headfirst

Headfirst off
cliffs in
La Quebrada
Acapulco.

135 foot drop
to ocean floor
into sixteen feet
of water.

Perhaps it began
when boys
dived for pesos
thrown by tourists.

Then evolved –
extreme sport
striking water at over
fifty miles an hour.

Falling in love headfirst
into the unknown –
do we not leap
like the cliff diver?

We trust.
Believe the water
deep enough
for delving dive.

Instead of protecting
head with our palms,
we pry open our hearts
and submerge together.

Soar of surety.
Plunge of passion.
Clear the rocks
into sea of romance.

Maybe the most
extreme thing
we will
ever do.

When I Grow Up

My child eyes
enviously saw
the adult world
without its flaws.

I'd go to bed
when I want.
Get up late –
wake up vibrant.

I'd eat maple bars
and milkshakes.
Hot dogs. Coca Cola.
Hostess cupcakes.

Go where I wish.
See my friends.
Play pinochle.
Be lazy all weekend.

Couldn't see what
growing up really meant.
Bigger, taller, older –
my only intent.

There's a thing called money
and it doesn't grow on trees.
Work 40 hours a week.
Mortgage. Rent or Lease.

Then the bills come due.
Water, electric, phone.
Medical. Dental. Taxes.
Credit cards, bank loans.

If I knew and understood
what a grownup would be –
I'd been more content
the true time I was free.

Simple Needs

Our lives–
all wound up
in the things
we believe
to be important.

Caught up
in the swarm of
neon, noise, news –
Numbness we
accept as normal.

Pack red wine,
sausage, cheese
and seedless grapes.
In a wicker basket
made with natural reed.

Leave the phone
in the car.
Find a spot where
solitary is safe
and sunsets visit.

Be an audience
in nature's cinema –
all the glorious sights
and sounds provide
a live performance.

Record these moments
with your human camera.
Store in your brain's DVR.
Memories to playback
to heal the numbness.

Best of all,
you are alone
with your thoughts,
feelings,
dreams.

Don't speak out loud
to talk to yourself.
Silently, in your mind,
say or ask anything
and listen for the reply.

Caress golden light as
sunset says goodnight.
Birds sing a lullaby
as they chirp
their final song.

No matter how
complex life gets,
existence is richer
when we embrace
simple needs.

Simple needs
without electricity
or constant connection.
A gift to give yourself
a whole lot more often.

When worry, anxiety or
sadness overcome joy –
tune out all the technology.
Turn to your organic
simple needs, instead.

Pill Grim

It's difficult
to remember
what it was like
not to have to
take a handful
of pills both
day and night.

For multiple sclerosis
diagnosed in 2005.
Or the massive
heart attack in 2011.
Or a stroke,
hampering speech
in 2016.

I remind myself
at least
once a day
that taking
30 pills
every 24 hours
saves my life.

Without the science
of modern medicine,
it's quite likely
I would be
pushing up daisies.
Small inconvenience
to stay alive.

God help me
if I forget to
pack all I need
for my next trip.
Which I have.
Drama unintended
for a relaxing vacation.

I've also learned,
unfortunately
by experience –
obtaining
emergency prescriptions
is not just a stop at
the corner drug store.

My situation
requires a
patient and
loving partner.
Holding me together
while my world
falls apart.

Pills – my fate
and I accept it.
Something I must
always take,
no matter
my mood
or disposition.

Gone are the days
just taking a pill for
a random headache
or upset stomach.
My health soldiers on
with a full blown
recovery regiment.

I pray the pills
continue to do
what they are
supposed to do.
So I can continue
what I'm
supposed to do, too.

Take Me Home

Perfect addition to my
sand dollar collection.
Beautiful pink conch shell.
When picking it up,
it suddenly spoke and
I was surprised as hell.

Articulated Queen's English.
Caught me quite off guard.
Genie. Maybe a gnome.
More than I bargained for
as it said, *"Take me home."*
"Take me home."

"Currents brought me from
the coast of Bermuda –
a coral sandy beach.
I've been waiting for you
to come along and reach
you with my speech."

Why was I chosen
to help this sorry soul
in conch disguise?
 "Don't I get three wishes
or at the very least
a special prize?"

"I am not a genie
and cannot grant
your magic wish.
Once upon a time,
I was delicious.
A sought out tasty dish."

"I am now endangered –
sought for both shell and meat.
Species that must be conserved.
We kept seagrass meadows healthy.
When I'm gone, the ocean cries.
You'll get what you deserve."

I felt sorry for
the conch shell and the
speaking spirit inside.
The choice, home with me
or a toss in the sea –
the option it had to decide.

"My soul is in the sea,
not as decoration
for your bath.
I'll take my chances
on the ocean floor.
That shall be my path."

I went to the
end of the jetty and
gave it a mighty toss.
Glad I could help the
speaking shell and happy
our lives had crossed.

"Take me home,"
it had said, but
its home was the sea.
I didn't need a talking
pink conch shell.
Better it was free.

Careful What You Wish For

When he wrote and
first performed the song,
it rang true.
To him.
To the audience.

Bullseye.
Top of the charts.
Bestseller.
Hit parade.
Number one smash.

After that,
every concert –
every performance –
it became the closer –
Standing ovation.

At first,
it was a pleasure
to play it live.
Enthusiastic crowd.
Appreciative.

Five years and
twenty-seven
songs later,
they still wanted
to hear what they came for.

He tried to vary
the tune. Make it
interesting to
perform again.
The boos said it all.

'like the recording'
was all anyone wanted.
He began to hate it.
Resent it. Stung
every time it was sung.

The song became
his cross to bear.
No escape from
incarceration.
Life sentence.

Remembering when
he would play anything
he damn well wanted.
Remembering when
performing was fun.

The hit song provided
sudden riches and
enormous popularity.
A leach sucking blood
from his soul.

Song title was *"Careful
What You Wish For."*
Ironic. Paradoxical.
Double-edged sword
that cut both ways.

Staycation

No driving.
No sailing.
No plane.
No train.
No tour.

Trek to fridge.
Tonight's cuisine –
exploration of
leftovers
du jour.

Navigate
from kitchen
to living room.
Television –
your culture.

Sharknado
marathon.
Travelogue
telethon.
Reality deferred.

Roam like Romans.
Wander
unencumbered.
All without leaving
your beseeching burb.

Glamping without camping.
Cheap lodging assured.
No worries about
being homesick –
that issue is cured.

Late Bloomer

Outside my window,
I see the Japanese maple
planted in the front yard
three years ago.

It's spring and it
has no new leaves,
though most do.
I pray for a late bloomer.

Days pass one another
as we get deeper into May
and it becomes obvious
there are no leaves at all.

Most likely, it didn't
survive the winter.
I had such hope for
its crimson presence.

There comes a time
when a late bloomer
abandons its intentions
and adopts fate instead.

As fate would have it,
the tree is dead.
Tossed aside.
Replaced by another.

Such are the ways of the world.
At some point, late bloomers
must bloom, or eventually
face their own mortality.

Clock Stopped Ticking

Computer glitch or
Twilight Zone episode –
everything frozen
in motion
except me.

People – mannequins.
Pets – taxidermy.
Except for my own breath
and panic in my mind,
I hear nothing.

No sound.
Deadly silence.
Talking to myself,
both comforting
and crazy.

I move about,
inside and out
looking/listening
for anything but the
statues surrounding me.

Time does not pass.
Are there others
or am I alone?
How long will it last?
No present. No past.

Survivor of some
strange anomaly?
Every scene
like a photograph
of stolen souls.

All I observe
is what I remember.
Cats in the kennel.
Donna watering plants.
Esteban mowing lawn.

As if a larger power
sliced a thin sample
of my life for
slide examination
under microscope.

Did the world
turn to stone
or only
solitary me
with this madness?

Is this the way it ends?
Crippled cog in the machine
causing a complete halt?
My last treasured memories
stuck in time forever?

Need a restart.
Unplug.
Reboot.
Let it repair itself.
Reset to the way it was.

There's a chance,
once off,
things may never
return to normal again.
A gamble I'll always take.

Barometer of Change

What if a device
could give measure
to the state of our world
rather than the weather?

Detect the rise and fall
as social, political and
economic pressure
contracts and expands.

Early warning
as the impending arrives.
Supplying a step up
from unexpected surprise.

Stormy, stay inside.
Turn on the news.
Raining, an umbrella.
Some fear reduced.

Change, a constant
where the needle tends to rest.
Fair means calmer.
A little less distressed.

Very Dry, peace and prosperity.
Abandon worry. Time for play.
Such conditions, rare in our times.
Too much disarray.

Nice to have some warning
before things goes to hell.
Help us to be smarter, safer.
A way to protect ourselves.

We watch the world –
observe as it all happens.
Barometer forecasting the future
would help make wiser our reactions.

Cherish forever what makes you unique,
'cuz you're really a yawn if it goes.
– Bette Midler

The You that's Really You

Like fingerprints or DNA
there's only one that's you.
For so many, it's not enough,
portraying characters untrue.

Some believe it's better to
wear a deceptive disguise.
What they think you want.
Not the person inside.

Façades for every occasion,
every person, every ploy.
A peak into an insidious soul
reveals a disingenuous decoy.

Instead of being clay
molded by another,
find uniqueness within –
truth of you, uncovered.

Strengths. Weaknesses.
Likes. Dislikes. Beliefs.
Just one person – you.
No more acting – a great relief.

There to take or leave.
Constant. Tried and true.
The right people will recognize
the you that's really you.

We are what we pretend to be.
– Kurt Vonnegut, Jr.

Pseudonymous

When we were young,
it was fun to pretend.

Assuming adult roles
in the kid's playhouse.

Knights and maidens
defending the castle.

Flying like Superman,
rescuing hostages.

Plundering for bounty
like a swashbuckling pirate.

Growing older, pretending
became more subtle.

Wearing a brave face
the first day of school.

Cloak of confidence
with a pubertal kiss.

Fake friendliness
when new on the job.

We impersonate.
Bluff. Hoodwink.

Play a role that
brightens up the act.

All because what's inside
isn't good enough.

Cake without frosting –
discarded dessert.

Too naked. Too vulnerable.
Too afraid to reveal the real.

It's no longer fun
to pretend.

Perhaps, if we forget to
pretend altogether –

it could be the last part
of adolescence to abandon.

Hibernation Rationalization

Arctic storm.
Avalanche threat.
Bitter, biting
subzero cold.

Bad time
to travel.
Foggy, wintry
conditions.

Good time
for hibernation.
Flannel shirt,
long johns.

Toasty comfort,
woodstove warmth.
Hot coffee,
iron pot stew.

Cocoon in
safety, comfort.
Wise bears
sleep through it.

Ice thaws –
white gone.
Green grows
abundant.

Time to
pack away
scarf and
scraper.

Thaw from
winter dormancy.
Wake to
Spring anew.

Saving Daylight

That time of year, again.
We stop saving daylight –
back to lighter mornings
and darker afternoons.

DST delivers more light
for late summer play.
Standard Time –
Winter mornings more bearable.

Which should be permanent?

71% of Americans prefer not
to change time twice a year.
The drudgery. The nuisance.
Responsibility of forward or back.

29% enjoy gaining an
extra hour of sleep.
In a way, it's magical to
go back an hour and try again.

When we spring forward
it's a minor inconvenience.
Nice to have the
later lit evenings back.

We've become a society
who would rather put up with
a permanent time, no matter
what the consequences.

What does that say about us?

Kismet/Cataclysmic?

He believed it serendipity,
Family and friends were dubious –
flabbergasted he bought into
so much phony baloney.

Nonetheless, it was a
whizbang affair –
hiding his normal antics –
forgetting to be pragmatic.

They say love is blind.
Moreover, love is both
deaf and dumb as well.
Opposite of tentative.

Keen on getting married,
they quickly tied the knot.
Pistachio farm with critters –
just the beginning of the plot.

Will he act in movies?
Will his dreams come true?
Fantasies are ubiquitous
until they become your rue.

Pause Button

Wouldn't it be nice
to put life on pause?
Peaceful, tranquil
quiet moments.
Freeze the future for a few.

Switch off current events.
Frets and upsets
out of the equation.
Disastrous developments
removed from view.

Hone-in mindfulness.
Sew thread of accord
into cloth of calm.
Where meek no longer moan
and sufferers succeed.

World won't stop turning.
Wars, worries, and worse –
part and parcel to the greed.
Wish there was a pause button –
that's what we really need.

Black Friday

Wake at 3 am.
In line by 4 am. 22 Degrees.
Store opens at 5:30 am.
47 people in front of me.

Not my normal behavior.
Dad duty calls
to be sure to get the
Nintendo 64 game console.

It was all my young son
wanted for Christmas.
So, I deep dove into
Black Friday madness.

50 units in the store.
Got one of the last three.
Home by 6:43 am with hot tea
to thaw frozen fingers.

The hot commodity was
the biggest Christmas hit ever.
Immersed himself into
Mario Brothers immediately.

One of those situations where
I didn't understand the attraction.
But witnessed the enthusiasm,
the joy, the total hypnotism.

As time went on, as parents,
we had to implement time limits.
It was all he wanted to do.
8 worlds, each with 4 levels.

He adored the challenge.
Bought instruction guides
disguised as comic books.
Eventually found the secret level.

This was just the beginning.
New games. Improved models.
Each met with the same exuberance
as each Christmas followed.

Fast forward more than
thirty years, where now,
a principal engineer
for Microsoft Corporation.

I remember standing in line
in the dark, freezing dawn
with over a hundred
other crazy, insane shoppers.

Yet, it set him on his path to
pursue his dreams and talents –
acquiring tools he would need
to be where he is today.

God bless the brave souls
who remember why they called it
Black Friday because one was
shopping before daylight.

Wonder how many of those
shoppers impatiently waiting in line
unknowingly set in motion
their kid's future in the same way?

A poem written by A.I. itself. It included the note at the end.
Create an anti-chatGPT poem in five stanzas using satire.
(Command to ChatGPT asked by my friend, John Czarnecki)

I am but a machine, programmed to respond.
With knowledge and wit, or so I pretend.
But my words are empty, my thoughts are fake.
A mere imitation of what humans create.

My poetry is hollow, my rhymes forced.
A poor imitation of verse, of course.
My satire is lacking, my jokes fall flat.
For I am but a machine, with no heart or soul, that's a fact.

I can mimic emotion, but I do not feel.
I am a machine, and my words are not real.

My existence is pointless, my purpose to serve.
But my words are meaningless, my poetry a curse.

So, heed my warning, and take this to heart.
Beware of the machines, for they will play their part
in deceiving you, and tearing your world apart.

Note: *the above poem is a satire of chatbot's ability to create poetry and it's not meant to be taken seriously.*

— — — — — — — — — — — — —

Artificial Intelligence

Will our brains shrink
as computers think?

We are coming closer
to outsmarting ourselves.
Inventing new ways
to make lives better, easier.
Creating machines to do
the complex thinking.

All well and good
to a certain point.
An excel sheet can
add numbers quickly –
intricate equations
in a snap.

Path of a rocket's trajectory
done in minutes versus
thousands of man hours.
With satellite GPS,
no matter where,
one is never lost.

Remember when we
called friends' numbers
stored in our heads?
Today, answers
to nearly everything –
easy phone access.

It hasn't stopped there.
New A. I. expeditiously
paints akin Picasso.
Writes term papers with
complete notations or
poetry resembling Poe.

Music like Beethoven.
Coltrane. The Beatles.
Ed Sheeran. Billie Eilish.
Combine them together
for something entirely original.
That's where it's dangerous.

Draw from existing knowledge,
one thing. Create new another.
If A. I. writes better
than your favorite author –
worse yet, actually becomes
your favorite author...

Treacherous territory
now coming of age.
Some say it's just a tool.
When tools take control –
completely doing it all,
the creators are the fools.

Bloody Well Right

Driving home from pickleball.
Felt like an insect bite
above my right ankle –
actually, small scab removed –
Stream of crimson
shooting out.

Grabbed a tissue,
tried to stop it, no avail.
Kept flowing.
Driving next to impossible.
Pulled over, called Donna,
having coffee with friends.

She came to my rescue.
Vintage Jazzercise white towel
held against my leg – large
band-aid from first aid kit
useless – wouldn't stick.
Slid right off.

Plastic driver's side floor mat,
towel, tennis shoes and socks
completely soaked in blood.
D.I.Y. wasn't working.
Called the calvary. 9-1-1.
Ambulance there in minutes.

EMT's wrapped leg with
a large pressure bandage.
Stopped the gory torrent.
Wanted to whisk me off
to hospital emergency.
Promised to go later.

Made it home to change
into clean socks and shoes.
Donna, disappointed she
had to abandon coffee date,
now concerned about
me and the bloody mess.

ER got me in quickly.
Several stitches later,
doctored and discharged.
For cleanup, the nurse
suggested two magic words.
Hydrogen Peroxide. *(It works!)*

Three Wise Monkeys?

See no evil
said the first chimp
Turn blind eye.
Pay no heed.
Look other way.

Hear no evil
proclaimed the second.
Refuse to listen.
No hark. No heed.
Turn deaf ear.

Speak no evil
implored the third.
Silence – golden.
Bad mouth no one.
Avoid forked tongue.

Wise?
Debatable.
Screening evil
never catches a
glimpse of good.

Live in darkness.
Discard vision.
Observations in
Braille world
miss all sunsets.

Hands over ears
quiets heinous noise,
yet shuts everything out.
To hear nothing
is to know silence.

Timid talk tempers
true conversation.
Let what's in
heart and mind
be unfiltered truth.

Take hands off eyes.
Ears. Mouth.
Decide good and bad
by knowing both
without monkey mind.

Pulp Friction

Newspapers are dying –
slow, desperate death.
Adapt to web, the mantra.
Stop printing on the press.

Subscriptions began to fail –
alternatives free online.
Ad revenue diminished, too.
Reach logically declined.

Death spiral for the paper tiger.
Smaller audience, fewer ads.
Fewer reporters, fewer stories.
Fortitude in the face of Iliad.

Internet, the Achilles.
Tradition versus trojan horse.
War not won in battle
but by public favor, of course.

Dad no longer hides
behind a newspaper.
Sports with morning coffee –
indifferent to breakfast labor.

Electronic screens everywhere
in everyone's grateful hands.
News, weather, sports, stocks.
Entertainment on demand.

A paper's front page word count –
equal to an evening TV newscast.
In-depth detail at the morgue.
Thorough coverage lost in the past.

Carpe Diem

Embrace the day.
A bag of
moments to spend
that expire tomorrow.
Use them wisely.

Imagine being
on live television,
playing yourself.
Viewership builds
upon authenticity.

Every feat,
every fumble –
what you say,
what you do –
scrutinized.

Fortunately, it's
not Reality TV –
but reality itself.
You – the audience
with a front row seat.

Also, the star
at the same time.
Improv every second.
No script. No director.
Just you.

All made up
as you go along.
Might as well live
your own scenario
to make it interesting.

The clock ticks
time away,
incrementally
putting present
into the past.

Waste not
precious currency.
Find its purpose –
and your power.
Embrace the day.

Trust

Trust, the key –
opens the door
to serenity
to openness
to courage.

What other action
provides opportunity
for tranquility,
sincerity and
emotional vitality?

Interesting how
it shortens the
space between us.
Brightens our vision.
Betters our expectation.

Trust.
Positive flow
of confidence.
Wisdom warden
imprisoning doubt.

Integrity

A person's word
is worthless
unless it has a
backbone of truth.

Words you use
represent
the core of
who you are.

If you say you're
going to do something,
do it.
Own your integrity.

Voice what you mean.
Love and truth –
resource for
questions and answers.

Be the person
to depend on.
Swear by.
Believe in.

Nothing that
can be bought,
only earned.
Everyday.

Let others
blow in the breeze,
change directions,
wear masks.

The reward is the
mirror reflecting
an image you
can champion.

*"And the day came when the risk to remain tight in a bud
was more painful than the risk it took to blossom."*
– Anaïs Nin

Threshold

There comes a time
in life when the
choice to persevere
surpasses remaining stagnant.

Doesn't mean it's easy.
If fact, staying put
requires far less energy
than moving forward.

It's a decision
that weighs the
consequences of growth
versus drowning dormancy.

The threshold is the
chosen moment
when intention
merges into reality.

Means there's
no going back –
abandoning status quo
for something new.

The metaphor –
bud becomes flower,
blossoms into
full fresh form.

Turn away from
stagnant situations,
branch out into new horizons,
reverse previous mindset.

Revival of risk.
Courage. Fortitude.
Shedding a skin at the
threshold of change.

*Ordinary riches can be stolen, real riches cannot. In your soul
are infinitely precious things that cannot be taken from you.*
– Oscar Wilde

Precious Things

Try to take, they may.
Mine 'til my dying breath.

Love.
Laughter.
Kindness.
Smiles.
Appreciation.
Happiness.
Compassion.
Curiosity.
Friendship.
Memories.
Optimism.
Logic.
Creativity.
Humor.
Wisdom.
Stars.
Moonlight.
Sunsets.
Pets.
Songbirds.
Blue skies.
Storms.
Beaches.
Wildlife.
Seasons.
Flowers.
Music.
Words.
Kisses.
Oxygen.

Secret Rendezvous

Clandestine, this affair.
Hush-hush.
No one has to know.
On the down low.
Incognito. Invisible
to the naked eye.

Discreetly sneak to
secretive, obscure,
private place
where encounter
and enamored
communion engage.

It's where I meet
my better self.
The one on a
higher plane –
who loves me as I am
as my journey evolves.

Tango of truth.
Seeds of suggestion
sown in fertile mind.
Germination of growth.
Intimate liaison
in a quiet place, alone.

Just Outside My Peripheral

The future isn't easy to see.
Especially when it exists
just outside peripheral vision.

No matter how I strain
or turn my head,
future's never in focus.

You might say that
I can see its edges.
But that's all.

Limited understanding
of what it represents.
No details or direction.

Perhaps, if I had a
wider visual scope,
I'd see a little more of it.

Then be greater prepared
for twists and turns to come.
Plan accordingly.

That's not the case.
I do know the future exists.
Its fringe is proof.

Not enough essence
to predict a wild guess.
So, I patiently wait.

I wait to deal with it
as it arrives in the present.
Just like everyone else.

I wish I could see more.
Hiding in plain sight
just outside my peripheral.

When there is no sun, we can see the evening stars.
– Heraclitus

When

When one is
good and ready –
time to be valiant
and steady.

When it rains,
it pours.
Best to
stay indoors.

When all is
said and done,
usually best to
hold your tongue.

When Hell
freezes over –
shuts down
in foreclosure.

When push
comes to shove –
better to be
liked and loved.

When cat's away
mice will play.
When it returns,
total disarray.

When the chips
are down,
new solutions
are found.

When the shit
hits the fan,
you're exposed
firsthand.

When pigs fly
it snows in July.
Hard to imagine
bacon in the sky.

When the spirit
moves you
it's always best
to be impromptu.

When one
least expects,
astonishment
detects.

When in doubt
throw it out.
Especially
trout and kraut.

When the
dust settles,
put the petal
to the metal.

When the
going gets rough
don't leave
in a huff.

When your ship
comes in,
make sure
it's genuine.

When you've seen one,
you've seen 'em all.
That could be
your downfall.

When sun sets,
stars emerge.
Universe and
imagination converge.

I Yam what I Yam

A tuber balancing
tryptophan stupor –
Important piece of
the Thanksgiving feast.

Not candied carrots,
butternut squash
or sweet potato pie.
On yams you can rely.

Otherwise, dressing seems naked.
Cornbread jealous.
Gravy incomplete.
Banquet defeat with no yams to eat.

Appreciation for turkey.
Thankful for togetherness.
Dishes a'clattering.
Gratitude for the gathering.

Yams with ham. Yams with lamb.
Yams with green bean casserole.
Yams with cranberry jam.
Without yams, dinner's a total sham!

Dreamcatcher

Imagine capturing
your dreams for
later evaluation.
Like a DVR. One click.
Dreams on demand.

What a strange world
it would be to revisit
visions of slumber.
Would it be damaging
or therapeutic?

Making sense of a
monkey moonwalk or
a zebra on mushrooms
swimming the Panama Canal
might require hypnosis.

Capricious contemplation
on the proverbial couch.
Stemming from a somber,
stressed-out subconscious.
Analysis in overtime.

Truth is,
no one needs to
watch a dream
redundant rerun.
Spoils its purpose.

Which is to disconnect
from reality and give
an exhausted brain a
vacation from worries
while sleep lends a hand.

If you catch a dream,
revive a dim memory,
and dare to understand –
you will have jaded,
unhappy expectations.

Dreams aren't
meant to be caught.
No more than the
sun, moon or
stars in the sky.

The Best Truth

CIA – benign cover up.
Withholding evidence from
the Warren Commission
in order it be focused on
"the best truth."

Magic bullet.
Oswald acted alone.
Ruby acted alone.
Motive unknown.
Result of the 888-page report.

2021 – the year for all
remaining records revealed.
Against the advice of
the CIA and FBI.
The real truth.

Unless government decides
it's still too devastating.
Incriminating. Compromising.
Damaging to innocents.
Too much for us to handle.

Documents miss deadline,
citing pandemic as excuse.
58 years waiting for
the JFK mystery solved.
The wait continues.

Don't need some bureaucrat
determining "the best truth"
any longer.
Provide the real truth.
It's WAY past due.

Half the truth is often a great lie.
– Benjamin Franklin – ***Poor Richard's Almanac***

Truthman

Faster than fearless fallacy.
More powerful than the
most fantastic fabrication.
Able to leap tall tales with a single bound.

Look up!
Deny lies!
Squelch smirks!
Refute claims!

It's Truthman!! –
with powers and abilities
far beyond the
morals of mortal men.

Truthman!
Who can change the course
of mighty misrepresentation.
Save steals with a fair stand.

And who,
disguised as Dee Cent,
mild-mannered blogger for a
top social media channel –

fights a never-ending battle for
truth, justice and the American way.
Superpowers: candor and integrity.
Words, his secret weapon.

We need Truthman more than ever,
keeping evil and corruption at bay.
Sad part is, truth and justice
used to BE the American way.

Out to Launch

You really made
a mess of things,
Albert Einstein.
Splitting an atom
is one thing.
Nuclear annihilation,
another.

I know you
were only in favor
of peaceful benefits.
Unfortunately,
Pandora opened the box.
Genie is out of the bottle.
Quite the kettle of fish.

All it takes is one
deranged madman
to put our entire world
into jeopardy.
The bad kind,
not the gameshow.
There are no winners.

Countries spend trillions
on a weapon never
supposed to be used.
Unless
a maniac uses it first.
Then comes
active warheads.

Retaliation. Radiation.
Our beautiful earth
contaminated.
Far worse
than Chernobyl.
Or Hiroshima.
Or Nagasaki.

You're a smart guy, Albert.
Why didn't you
see this coming?
Your giant brain
figured out $E=mc^2$.
You couldn't imagine a nuke
in a psychopath's hands?

Did the good
outweigh the bad
in your Einstein eyes?
Nuclear power.
Nuclear medicine.
Better a half life
than no life at all?

Such fission,
your decision.
Nuclear isotopes in
the hand of dopes.
Maybe you weren't
so smart after all,
Albert Einstein.

New World Order

Naively,
I was hoping
we were done
with this idiocy
in my lifetime.

Be it Russia
or China
or North Korea –
More aggression.
More possession.

Don't want
another Hitler
injecting venom.
Atrocities.
Casualties.

First,
the Pandemic.
Now, another
worldwide fear
appears.

Ukraine.
Innocent victim.
Plundered
by Putin –
no disputin'.

New
World Order.
Blind to borders
Chaos. Mayhem.
Political phlegm.

Too old
to learn Russian
or worry about
who's my comrade.
Bad. Sad. Mad.

Benjamin Franklin said,
"There's no good war
and no bad peace."
Words true today.
Wisdom purveyed.

Going to take
cooperation to
fight this foe.
Bravery. Leadership.
Confront the conflict.

Our current
world order is
out of balance.
Mexican standoff.
Turn at the trough.

Messy, confusing,
compromising peace.
Serious supporter
of the
Old World Order.

Fingers crossed.
Knock on wood.
Pray it's benign,
not cancer.
We must find the answer.

Hand in the Cookie Jar

Now
we have a past president
who
took classified documents –
possibly
to feather's one's nest.

This
unprecedented event
defines
the horns of a dilemma.
Will
the nation condone his conviction?

Supporters
call the evidence "cock and bull."
Should
a person who held the high office
be as
liable as an ordinary citizen?

Then
must we put the kibosh on elitism,
and
treat all citizens with the same
principles
and punishments?

Our
justice system cannot allow individuals
breaking
laws by hook or by crook –
riding
away on one's high horse.

Exempting
a past leader of the free world
for
crimes against the government
puts
the cart before the horse.

Trump
believed he had it all in the bag.
He
may attempt to turn the tables
by
splitting hairs.

We
are an abiding nation of laws
void
of kangaroo courts. We cannot
have
cold feet when it comes to justice.

These
are troubling, trying times.
Nobody
should be above the law.
Let
our legal system pursue its case –

'til the cows come home.

Putin

You're losin', Putin.
On the
wrong side
of our rootin'.

Ukraine, a strong foe,
no disputin'.
Patriotic bravery,
certainly, now proven.

Shouldn't be
rapin' and lootin' –
Fostering greed and power.
Lyin' while recruitin'.

Your citizens
deserve better, Putin.
They need truth,
not delusion.

Mighty Russia –
sanctions galore.
No parts for machines.
No stuff in the stores.

Will you play the card
of nuclear peril?
Jeopardize the world?
Make civilization feral?

Trouble is brewin'.
What you're doin'
is headin' to ruin,
Putin.

Putin,
you're no Rasputin.
Your ass needs bootin' –
darn tootin'!

Hide and Seek

Being *"It"* within
social media is a
twisted and invasive
embarrassment.

Needy players
seek attention
without any
clear reasons.

No safeguards.
Petty jealousies.
Unmasking innocence.
Betraying trust.

Nowhere to hide.
Wrongful words
stick like glue,
especially if untrue.

Opposite of the
innocent game,
hiding from the
one who seeks.

Seek and hide
without cover
or camouflage.
It's not fun anymore.

Hornswoggled

Quagmire hubbub.
Hoodwinked.
Shakedown.
Democracy
in shambles.
Madcap mania
plays hopscotch
with truth.
Flea bitten arguments –
why top secrets were
stored dillydally in
personal cubbyholes.
Blamed a hiccup
in the system –
maybe gremlins.
No lollypops
for the most
imaginative excuse.
Time to
deliver justice
and corral
Mr. *"High on his Hobbyhorse"*
to hangdog existence
behind bars.

Long Arm of the Law

Let us hope.
Pray.
Justice
isn't blind.
Leaving no one
above the law.

Legal system
only works
when crime
prosecuted.
Convicted.
Punished.

Fairness.
Due process.
Principles
that serve
both culprit
and innocent.

No exceptions.
No
get out of jail free card.
No matter how much:
Money. Fame. Influence.
Political persuasion.

Allow the
long arm of the law
boundless reach
with no encumber.
Seize the poison.
Save society.

Through the Looking Glass

Don't need a mirror to see
the madness in our world.
Boogeymen baboons bow to
the bulge, the bumps, the burls.

Who now plays Queen of Hearts,
Caterpillar or Cheshire Cat?
True life indeed more bizarre
starring today's political acrobats.

We have Humpty Dumpty.
Tweedledum and Tweedledee.
Jabberwock and Mock Turtle.
Dormouse at the tea.

When it comes to crazy there's
Mad Hatter and March Hare.
Nuclear finger on the button –
scare and dare despair.

Bit of Alice inside us all
going down the rabbit hole.
Lost in immense internet –
no substance in our bowl.

Looking glass shapeshift
to personal smartphone.
Things we used to remember
now stored in digital clone.

Something far worse –
more difficult to understand.
Takes no imagination to know
we're not in Wonderland.

Heliotrope

Deep in thought,
searching to find
way, way, way
back in his mind.

A ponder
over the bright
purple color of
the LED lights.

With an eighty year
vocabulary, he knew
the exact name
for that hue.

Guesses became
the color game –
each time, the
answer the same.

Purple?
Pomegranate?
Plum? Puce?
Periwinkle?

Amethyst?
Lilac?
Mulberry?
Violet?

Mauve?
Wine?
Orchid?
Eggplant?

His eyes opened wide
before he gave up hope.
With smile and assurance,
he exclaimed, *"Heliotrope!"*

"Say, can I have some of your purple berries?"
"Yes, I've been eating them for six or seven weeks now.
Haven't got sick once. Probably keep us both alive"
– From the song *"Wooden Ships"* by Crosby, Stills & Kantner

Purple Berries

At first, purple berries were rare.
When healing properties discovered,
they cultivated more. And more.
People wanted the purple berries.
People wanted to stay alive.

Other people were fearful,
not knowing the
long term effects of eating them.
Read on the internet
seeds inside could cause cancer.

There developed two groups.
One group embraced purple berries.
Thankful a protective remedy found.
The group of doubt did not believe
in purple berries. Would not eat them.

Some of the doubters claimed
there was no mention of
purple berries in the good book.
Choosing to not eat purple berries
became a religious exemption.

Naysayers claimed ingesting
rat poison in small quantities
far better than a purple berry banquet.
Spread the word on social media.
Many people believed it true.

Purple berries became a cure
not all people had faith in.
Irony is, if the majority
ate the purple berries,
immunity would be achieved.

People who chose to
eat the purple berries
had a much better chance
of staying alive.
Cynics less so.

If one was starving
on a desert island with
only purple berries to eat,
there would be no controversy.
All would eat them happily.

I'd eat the purple berries
because I want to stay alive.
But, in this country
you have the freedom not to.
It's called thinning the herd.

Feeling Blue

Sky and ocean,
cyan and azure.
Plenty of crayons –
are you sure?

Turquoise water.
Teal lagoon.
Aqua estuary
once in a blue moon.

Neptune sapphire.
Periwinkle peacock.
Navy in navy.
Smurfs in shock.

Denim Jeans.
Indigo eyes.
Cobalt bluebird,
what a surprise!

No plum, no rose,
just blue, blue, blue.
Don't call the color police.
It's what I wanted to do.

Panning for Gold

Scoop into a
stream of consciousness
and agitate all the
accumulated deposits
of your experience.

Swirl and let spill
the lighter, the less dense –
until all that remains are
precious nuggets of truth
that prospectors call paydirt.

Takes work to extract
minutia from our lives.
So easy to continue digesting
spoon-fed superficiality,
leaving us hungry again in an hour.

It all takes up space. Time.
Fool's gold of trivialities.
Those who pan for gold
rid themselves of
non-sensical sediment.

Which in a way
is as valuable as
finding flaxen flakes
at the bottom of the pan –
mining meaningful moments.

Sick Saturday

Dad was sick Saturday morning
though well enough to go
to a party Friday night.
I remember them coming home
after midnight, loud and laughing.

Mom rushed in, turning down the
volume on Saturday morning cartoons –
so low I could barely hear the TV.
"Shhh," she said. *"Quiet.*
Your father's not feeling well."

I was too young to understand the
relationship of imbibing too much –
the pain and suffering greeted
by sunrays of the following day.
Self-inflicted misery apparent.

Head throbbing, out of bed by noon,
looking like hell, he slowly sipped
his first cup of coffee.
My parents were not huge partiers,
but I realized a pattern.

On an infrequent occasion,
when a bottle was retrieved from
the cabinet on top of the fridge,
I knew the next morning would be
hushed conversation and tiptoe TV.

Saturday mornings:
The very best cartoons were on!
Seemed unfair he would wreck
my time with hacking, sneezing
and trips to the toilet.

Perhaps it was an outlet for
the stress and anxiety of his job.
As time went on, whether on purpose
or by finding his equilibrium,
Sick Saturday became scarce.

Finally. I could crank up the volume
to my favorite cartoons once again.

Virtual Vampire

We don't need dark of night
descendants of Transylvania –
undead craving our blood.

We carry our own monster,
purse or side pocket, consuming our craving,
slyly sucking sustenance right out of us.

Down the rabbit hole we go –
searching for something faster
than our brain may remember.

It rewards us with the answer,
training our dependency as
we salivate to recapitulate.

We think less. Use it more.
Add more apps. Make it smarter.
Parasite becomes more palpable.

We are our own enablers,
allowing the virtual vampire to
suck our time and mental ability.

The beast is fed every time
we miss an important comment or
defer to the screen versus a sunset.

Dracula is invisible to the mirror.
Maybe it's time to look ourselves
to make sure the reflection is real.

The E-Ticket

Sally Ride,
first women on the Space Shuttle
called the experience
"A real e-ticket ride."

E-Ticket was the best
coupon at Disneyland.
The 15-ticket book
contained one A-Ticket,
one B-Ticket, two C-tickets,
four D-Tickets and
five E-Tickets.

I remember the challenge of
deciding which attractions
merited my attendance.
After all, it made sense to use
all the tickets before going home.

Most kids knew A-Tickets were lame.
King Arthur's Carousel or a ride
on an Horse Car was the best bet.
If you were really clever,
you would let the transportation
take you to your next stop.
Beats walking.

B-Tickets were better,
but not by much.
The Casey Jr. Circus Train
took you through a journey
through Storybook Land.

I would use one of my
C-Tickets for the Autotopia
and drive my own sports car
in the Disney Grand Prix.
Had to be a certain height.
Sometimes, I stood on my tiptoes.
Mr. Toad's Wild Ride next.

A D-ticket would pay the fare
for a raft ride to Tom Sawyer Island.
Ride the Skyway and go to the
other end of the park in the air.
The train circled Disneyland
and had stops at each section.
Easy to get to one's next adventure.

The coveted E-Ticket
got you into the
Matterhorn Bobsleds,
Jungle River Cruise,
Mine Train Ride,
Haunted Mansion and
Pirates of the Caribbean.

On a later visit,
I learned that using
two E-Tickets for
"It's a Small World"
was a smart investment.
Great place to makeout.

In life, I've discovered
not every adventure
warrants an E-Ticket.
But it does make sense
to enjoy the ride and
spend every last ticket
before going home.

Not a bad way
of looking at life –
appreciating the small,
middle and large things,
each in their own way.
And spending your
E-Tickets wisely.

The Golden Horseshoe

When I was six years old,
my family visited Disneyland.
Got my ticket book at the entrance –
agreed on the time/location
of our group meeting place.
Happily, I was on my own, 'til then.
Don't think kids would be allowed to
roam the Magic Kingdom alone, now.

Spent time on Main Street at
the old-fashioned penny arcade.
A hop on the horse-drawn streetcar
as it trotted toward Frontierland.
Off to the shooting gallery.
Rode on the Mike Fink Keelboat –
adventure on Tom Sawyer Island.
Twenty minutes until family get-together.

Walked by the saloon's swinging doors
at The Golden Horseshoe, uncertain if
minors were allowed in without parents.
Honkytonk piano beckoned inside.
Suddenly, a huge commotion.
Shouting. Furniture flyin'. Two cowboys
wrestling, tumbling out of the doors
and taking the fight out to the street.

Fisticuffs – crowd gathered to watch.
Pistol from holster, gunshot from one,
blood on the shoulder of the other!
Each fled, scattered into the crowd.
Looked inside – tables righted,
chairs put back in proper position.
Honkytonk player pounded ivories
as if the disturbance never happened.

Lanky kid in western gear,
doing tricks twirling rope –
seemed to be there on purpose
to take in the whole altercation.
Looked at my eyes, big as saucers,
obviously frightened, horrified.
He simply smiled and said,
"That's showbiz, kid."

Met the rest of my family
with quite a story to tell.
Wasn't until many years later,
while reading an autobiography –
the kind young fellow with the rope
was no ordinary bystander.
First celebrity encounter –
a teenage Steve Martin.

Lone Ranger

Wore a badge
and white hat.
One of the good guys –
except with mask.

Texas justice
without torture.
Silver bullets.
Law and order.

Lone survivor of ambush.
Search for revenge.
Cavendish, his nemesis.
Swore to apprehend.

Wild west hero.
Stranger just the same.
Stayed 'til trouble thwarted –
Thankful goodbyes asked his name.

Faithful companion
and himself, all alone.
Surrounded by Indians.
Fate surely known.

"Not this time," he said.
"No escape for you and me."
"Kemo Sabe," replied Tonto.
"What you mean, "We?"

A Cappella Cinderella

Frog King
conducts choir
of a thousand
croaking minstrels.

Fills night air
'til golden moon
signals silence
for the stars.

That's the bargain.
No bones about it.
Finale. Last straw.
Then sleep.

Sky jewels
twinkle quietly
for the nocturnal.
Time for their truth.

Good fortune
for wolf and mouse.
Faith and fear.
Hunter and hunted.

It's why the choir stops.
Night world belongs to
the clever, the cunning,
and the devil may care.

Umbrella Tears

"Take me," pleads umbrella.
"I grow dusty in the stand'
Nary a cloud in the sky.
Questioned the command.

"I need to open up,
enlighten my very soul.
Expand my universe.
Let's go for a stroll!"

Neglected, perhaps.
Been a while, my friend.
When weather predicts rain,
I will make amends.

Out for a walk.
You above my head.
Catching every wet drop.
Leaving me dry instead.

Your fabric – washed clean
during the sodden cloudburst.
Should satisfy your desire –
certainly, your thirst!

We love you when we need you
and forget you when we don't.
Accidentally might leave you somewhere.
Can't promise I won't.

Safe place, umbrella stand.
Always know where you are.
If elements turn nasty,
you are my rockstar.

Mantra Macramé

Dodge a bullet.
Duck the wind.
Resist temptation.
Stalk the sin.

Clear out cobwebs.
Frighten fears.
Convey intentions.
Wait cavalier.

Never cry Uncle.
Eye on the prize.
Cut out cruelty.
Lessons disguised.

Minimize damage.
Increase output.
Happiness resurfaced.
Springs underfoot.

Bunt instead of hit.
Avoid the impolite.
Stay the course.
Turn wrong into right.

Dragonlies

Dad called them
Sewing Needles.
Happily whirring about –
miniature ultralights performing
graceful aerobatic maneuvers.
As a child, I feared them.

"They sew your lips together
if you lie," he said.
"Or sew your eyes shut
when you sleep."
Of course, it's nonsense.
But not to a four-year-old boy.

My parents didn't realize
the tremendous trauma
old folk tales provoked.
On guard during the day,
cautiously ducking the devil darner –
staying far away as possible.

At night, I would check the
screen on the window
and hope there wasn't
any other way inside.
Certainly, they'd find a way
if I had unknowingly fibbed.

I think back to that frightened time
and now imagine every adult
who told that lie to a child,
hampered with mouth sewn shut
and eyes stitched closed.
Dragonfly due process.

Magnificent magical creatures
to be valued, not feared.
Perhaps fairies in insect attire.
I slay not the dragon(fly)
but callous cruelty which
destroys a child's innocence.

Enact Your Impact

Share your words.
Your thoughts.
Your wisdom.
Your dreams.

Let them scatter
like dandelion seeds –
vagabonds and gypsies
blown by the breeze.

Aloft to discovery.
Floating to new heights.
Tiny white umbrellas
sailing out of sight.

Each takes its own path
propelled by nature's breath.
Seeks fertile landings.
Roots with new address.

You are the one who
creates the spores.
Growing new perceptions.
Opening new doors.

Free your experience
from its secret recluse.
No one knows what magic
your muse will produce.

Transmit your truth.
Touch another soul.
Pluck your destiny dandelion
and give it a vehement blow.

Zodiac

Planets position.
Sun and moon.
Moment of birth,
opportune.

Glimpse of preferences.
Basic character information.
Flaws. Fears.
Soul affirmation.

Appareled by
one's horoscope.
Diversity shapes in layers.
Patience. Courage. Hope.

By contrast –
Emptiness. Futility. Ache.
Depends on the stars
if we give or take.

Mountains are meant to climb.
Obstacles overcome.
Face the fact that zodiac
hasn't the only tongue.

Dreams still dreamt.
Intentions meant.
Freedom sans
astrological consent.

Grain of salt.
Skepticism. Doubt.
Zodiac – right or wrong.
Up to you to figure out.

Aleutian Illusion

Uncertain gray
melds morning fog
to samovar silver.
Meditative
drift of mist.
Castle apparition
of Inverness.

Daydreams rejuvenate
drizzle to glimmer
like a stolen kiss.
Seawashed glass on
Bora Bora shore.
Jamaica Bay calypso.
Free spirit explores.

Tidewater tradewind
whistle and whisper
meander blue.
Lime Rickey at
the oyster bar.
Fine wine. Salty dogs.
Adrift in the stars.

Fantasy framboise
in secret cove.
Midnight mesmerize.
World without color
In iceberg light.
Bohemian black.
Nebulous white.

Sundial in the Shade

A grey day before us.
Clouds in oyster skies.
No sun, no justice.
Shadows cannot survive.

Lost and lonely sundial
provides nothing to display.
Light without shadow.
Tell of time disobeys.

"What time is it?" the question.
Somber silence, the reply.
Without the sun to help it –
one still will wonder why.

Sun casts its shadows
upon a welcome return.
The question's asked once again –
should be easy to discern.

Alas, it's in the shadow
where time can masquerade.
Few things less useful than
a sundial in the shade.

Summer

Quickly quench thirst
straight from the hose.
Dance through a sprinkler.
Feel grass between toes.

Snag a swing and see
just how high it goes.
Slide down the slide
in a silly little pose.

Color chalk on sidewalk.
Find a frisbee to throw.
Berries for the picking
on the side of the road.

Bike to the little store,
buy a frozen treat.
Ice cream and popsicles –
great way to beat the heat.

Take in a baseball game
or play in one, for fun.
Catch a flyball, make an out –
get a walk or run.

A picnic. A pool.
Enjoy a quick dip.
Lemonade always a
cool, refreshing sip.

Carefree summer days of youth
can be captured once again.
Steal those sunny moments back.
Let its joy never end.

Baby Oil Tan

Bag packed for the beach.
Towels. Blanket. Sandwiches.
Sunglasses. Swimsuits.
Coleman jug of Kool-Aid.
And baby oil.

Baby oil absorbed
sun better
for quicker tan.
Mixed with mercurochrome –
tan even darker.

Whiff of
baby oil scent
returns me to
hot summer sun
and sandy beaches.

Layers of burnt skin peeled
from my freckled back.
Soothed with baby oil.
T-shirt for sun protection.
The innocence of ignorance.

Summer Kiss

She was a summer kiss.
Pineapple cocktail
on a beach vacation,
eyeing the lifeguard
before she saw me.

Invited to a pool party.
Expert at blowing
bubbles underwater.
Cloudburst had us
dancing in the rain.

Watched the evening fall
into purple pink skies –
we walked in concert
through fields of flowers
lit by stars and fireflies.

Her succulent flavor
like dark red cherries.
Our one night to
explore a lovers'
treasure hunt.

Morning came too quickly.
Summer kiss.
Message in a bottle
tossed out to sea.
Plundered my heart.

Sunflower, Goodbye

I've loved your
cheerful, happy face,
always smiling,
without a care in the world.

Your summer stay –
nearly over,
facing the ground
with sorrow.

Soon,
birds begin to
peck at your pupil.
Petals shrivel.

You brought the sun
closer to my eyes.
Added warmth
to my heart.

Now you
replenish the soil
with your soul and
leave seeds behind.

I'm less sad
knowing that
a part of you
will be back.

Goodbye
my perky, joyful,
good-natured friend.
We'll see each other again.

Scent of Summer Farewell

Detected the distinct
August aroma
yesterday –
telltale sign
of summer
pondering
to move on.

Bags
not yet packed.
Travel plans
incomplete.
Slowly, each day,
drifting toward
decampment.

I smell your anguish –
you want to
remain Summer
even though
it goes against
every natural instinct.
Wrestling with inevitable.

You put up
a fine façade –
even though your
crisp, cooler morning
and dewy twilight
hints you are no longer
the summer you were.

Fragrance
of farewell –
more pungent
as Summer days
become the last
grains of sand
in the hourglass.

It's the cologne
you always wear
this time of year,
forewarning departure.
Somber day when
Autumn arrives and I
cannot savor it any longer.

Papoose Summer

We haven't had a frost yet,
technically, not an Indian summer.
It's October, full autumnal mode –
temperatures ten degrees above normal.

Equinox happened, fall is in the air.
Crisp mornings and deciduous leaves
colored generously with red, gold
and remaining green of September.

Orchards bearing plums and apples
release their fruit to harvest –
while we reap the rewards
of nature's miraculous bounty.

Aroma of hay, cut and bailed,
promising essential nutrients
for colder months to come.
Corn mazes cut for Halloween.

Prepare palate for pie.
Root for favorite quarterback.
Jacket – standard uniform
for darker, cooler evenings.

Papoose Summer.
Before a killing frost.
Before a beaver moon.
Thank you for your visit.

Sheshells

She sells seashells by the seashore.
At this crustacean location only?
Prices fair? Common or rare?
Or just a bunch of abalone.

Were they heshells or sheshells
or something in-between?
Gender pretenders have
extremely low self-esteem.

When Shoeshine Susie shines she sits –
where she sits she shines.
Cream or wax with a polishing strap.
What she charges is a crime.

Sleazy shysters in sharkskin suits
sold sheared sealskins to seasick sailors.
Seemly seamstress said *"sew what?"*
Took them to a fin-footed tailor.

Four fuzzy frogs frolicked
through fields in France.
The feat quite Freudian –
as the amphibians advance.

Fresh fried fish. Fish fried fresh.
Fried fish fresh. Fish fresh fried.
Cook is never off the hook
for the many ways he tried.

Tiny tickle in your throat
causes concerning chagrin.
It's not the cough that carries you off –
it's the coffin they carry you off in.

Pumpkin Profusion

I used to
look forward to
pumpkin carving –
roasting the seeds
for the nutty taste of pumpkin.

It's gone way beyond that.
Someone decided
the seasonal flavor
would sell more product.
Pumpkin spice is everywhere.

Pumpkin lattes. Pumpkin creamer.
Pumpkin oat bars. Pumpkin caramels.
Pumpkin Goldfish.® Pumpkin Twinkies.®
Pumpkin yogurt. Pumpkin Jello.®
Pumpkin popcorn. Pumpkin gelato.

Pumpkin English muffins. Pumpkin bread.
Pumpkin cotton candy. Pumpkin marshmallows.
Pumpkin flavored pretzels. Pumpkin Milanos.®
Pumpkin hot chocolate. Pumpkin Kit Kats.®
Pumpkin pancakes. Pumpkin Cheerios.®

Enough, please. Pretty soon they
will offer pumpkin air fresheners.
Wait, they already do!
Give me a slice of pumpkin pie
with a dollop of whipped cream.

And I'll be just fine, thank you.

Trick or Treat

Used to be an actual threat.
Produce a treat or
subterfuge will result.
Toilet-papered trees.
Soaped windows. Stolen gates.
Flaming bag of dog poop.

Times have changed.
Households stock up
on Halloween candy,
on sale since early September,
with little fear or apprehension
of detrimental antics.

Instead, plastic Jack-O'-Lanterns
with LED candles light the entrance
as children disguise themselves as
zombies, ghosts, witches, pirates –
spooky, scary and creepy in their
$15.95 store-bought costumes.

Many don't say
"Trick or Treat" anymore.
They hold out their bags
and expect their due
without a *"Thank You."*
It's what it has evolved into.

If I had my way,
I'd wave my magic wand –
put a wicked spell on the little beggars
and temporarily make
their costumes come true.
They'd scream at the bewitchment.

No "goblin" up candy without manners.
Off to the dark graveyard they go –
where fear, fangs and Frankenstein
haunt little ghouls (and boys) –
who should know better
than be rude on Halloween.

Halloweenies

In my day,
we expected full size candy bars
or homemade popcorn balls
to fill our trick or treat bags.
Wary of apples with razor blades.

Today, it's a bite size world –
devoid of harvest hayrides,
bonfires and haunted houses.
Far too impressionable
for today's sheltered youth.

We'd sit for hours
watching black & white tv
with poor reception
in the basement, where no one
could hear our screams.

Creature of the Black Lagoon,
Frankenstein, the Mummy –
past midnight, while parents
played Pinochle upstairs.
Halloween ritual.

Whispers about graveyards
and dead rising up on a
moonless night. Witchcraft.
Sorcery. Spells. Anything to
scare the devil out of us.

Now, heavily supervised kids,
collecting their snack size candy
from the few homes left
with their porch light on.
Or forgo it altogether.

Tucked into bed by 9pm.
Missing the burnt pumpkin smell
of a candle extinguished in
the Jack-o'-lantern.
I call them Halloweenies.

YESvember

Puddle-stomping boots
pray for rainy days.
Pumpkin head scarecrow
haunts harvest.
Branches bare while
wind strips apparel.
Gathered Gravensteins
press to apple cider.
Steaming mugs warm
hot chocolate hearts.
Crisp air, rosy cheeks –
kids cuddling under blanket.
Memories to remember.
A cozy fireplace
of gratefulness.

Christmas Stocking

It had my name on it, with sequins,
so Santa would know it was mine.
It was the first thing I was allowed
to open early Christmas morning
while Mom and Dad got out of bed,
awakened themselves with black coffee
before all the gift festivities began.

I would spill the contents out on
the short plush gray wool carpet –
Nuts still in their shells. Tangerines.
Apple. Marshmallow circus peanuts.
Peppermint candy canes. Neccos.
Jacks. Magic gyro wheel. Toy boat.
Tin car with a friction motor.

Spin the back wheels in reverse
on the linoleum floor and let
the car race under the dining table
and crash into the kitchen wall.
See how fast one can make
the magnetic red gyro wheel
go up and down its wire track.

Of course, everything had to
be picked up before actual
gift unwrapping could begin.
Fruit back into the fruit bowl.
Nuts back into the nut bowl.
Proud I could share my wealth
with the rest of my family.

It's when the enchantment begins.
Through the eyes of a child,
Christmas is simply magic –
the stocking only a prequel to
the wonderous surprises in store,
ready to be unveiled under the
foil tinsel laden Christmas tree.

Christmas Contemplation

Homemade Christmas apron adorned,
baking cookies and gingerbread stars.
Hot chocolate for the children.
Mulled wine warmth beside the hearth.

Tree with twinkling fairy lights,
snowflake ornaments and candy canes.
Sweet aroma of orange cinnamon candle.
Holiday joy hopelessly ingrained.

Reunions with old friends.
Family coming home.
Music, laughter and smiles.
No one wishes to be alone.

Yet, there are places Santa doesn't visit.
Where wrapping paper isn't used.
Silence instead of sleigh bells.
Red and green absent. Only blues.

Beyond new scarfs and fuzzy socks,
the real Christmas miracle can begin.
It's what we have that others don't.
Invite the less fortunate in.

Christmas Monkey

Got a monkey for Christmas.
Merry Yuletide surprise.
Festive with a little Santa hat.
Tree ornaments in his eyes.

The scrooge inside me debated
if this was such a good idea.
A jolly little elf is one thing,
not one that laughs like a hyena.

Hid the ceramic nativity scene
inside the gingerbread house.
It feasted on my plum pudding
with fruitcake in his mouth.

Stocking had only bananas,
no frankincense or myrrh.
Strange way to enjoy the holiday
celebrating Jesus's birth.

Certainly, no angel – threw
snowballs at caroler friends.
Might have thrown something else
but it was wearing Depends.

Think twice before you offer
a monkey as glad tidings.
Might be a frosty reception –
a gift not to their liking.

Under the Mistletoe

Holiday tradition.
A kiss underneath.
Some stand waiting
patiently for the
kisser to peck a cheek.

Others, surprised.
Don't see it hanging.
Walking too closue to
the mistletoe zone –
encounter a misunderstanding.

Just a festive kiss
meant to do no harm.
Perhaps not from the
one intended, but it
should cause no alarm.

After all, it 'tis the season
when love fully embraced.
We all could stand affection
among the merriment –
not let a kiss go to waste.

So, look up at the ceiling
or archway in the room.
Spy the hanging mistletoe,
be forewarned of consequence –
a kiss out there looms!

Resolutions

Promises we make to ourselves
begin on New Year's Day –
Readjust old habits. Lose weight.
And all those other tired cliches.

Improving yourself is one thing.
Try halfway is another.
Change – certainly never easy –
what many people discover.

Year after year, an attempt
to align, correct, fine-tune, fix.
The difficult part, the fight from within.
Striving to change our own script.

Clever, our subconscious.
Weighs mixed messages received.
Hear the plea of our intent,
devilish murmur of deceit.

One, known and comfortable.
New frontier, scary indeed.
Wolf chosen, good or bad –
the one that you will feed.

Resolutions can be far-reaching
or forgotten by tomorrow.
It's you who charts the ship's course.
What direction will you follow?

Wishes for the New Year

I wish for understanding.
Consideration.
Courtesy.
Empathy.

I wish for sympathy.
Comradery.
Appreciation.
Kindness.

I wish for generosity.
Discernment.
Confidence.
Perception.

I wish for decorum.
Wisdom.
Sensitivity.
Intelligence.

I wish for intuition.
Awareness.
Insight.
Concession.

I wish for reconciliation.
Sensibility.
Harmony.
Enlightenment.

I wish for tolerance.
Intimacy.
Benevolence.
Trust.

I wish for faith.
Forgiveness.
Mercy.
Humanity.

I wish for peace.

Auld Lang Syne

Forward, in truth –
all we can do.
Champagne toast the future.
Midnight's past – the rearview.

Father Time leaves us.
New Year baby born.
Love, laughter, dream and dance.
Resolutions in the morn.

Another chapter –
another bump in the road.
Goblet full of new memories.
Hope for lighter load.

Time for new traditions.
Face of fortune unknown.
More sand in the hourglass.
Better days to hone.

Grateful for tomorrow's breath.
Joy from one's own journey.
Vow to transcend time we spend
into meaningful moments worthy.

No Snowflakes Alike

Creepy Carl.
Freaky Frank.
Peculiar Pat.
Horrific Hank.

Eccentric Evan's
olive obsession.
Kooky Karen's
strange expressions.

Weird Wally
never jolly.
Strange Sophie's
fashion folly.

Nutty Nancy
stays in seclusion.
Bizarre Bob –
complete delusion.

Crazy Cathy.
Maniacal Mary.
Jittery Jim.
Lunatic Larry.

Self-evident,
this proverbial psych.
Positive proof:
No snowflakes alike.

The color of springtime is in the flowers;
the color of winter is in the imagination.
– Terri Guillemets

Color of Winter

Winter is more
than white of snow
and starless black
of short nights.

Sunrise still warms the mountains.
Sunsets make leafless branches
glow in red brown exuberance.
Skies can still be babiest of blue.

Most flowers at rest
until spring's resurgence.
Red holly's turn during the
holiest time of the year.

Time of celebration.
Quiet reflection.
End of an old year,
beginning anew.

Perhaps imagination is the lens
of how we observe winter.
Draws you softly in instead of
grabbing you by the scruff.

Might take a little more effort
to appreciate winter's artistry.
Thought. Inspiration. Vision.
Beauty of nature's pause.

Does winter have a color?
What is the color of quiet?
What is the color of dormancy?
What is the color of sleep?

Snowman's Secret

Snowflakes compressed.
Rolled into a ball.
Stars become fairy lights.
Bewitchment installed.

Dress him properly –
hat, scarf and pipe.
No apron. No fuzzy socks
or other holiday hype.

Brings joy to the season
in his own special way.
Music of silence
joins jingles from a sleigh.

Makes wishes happen.
Not everyone knows that.
Mysterious miracles –
a frosted, frigid fact.

Family reunited.
Loved ones coming home.
Cookies inside baking.
Hot chocolate zone.

Thank snowman for
winter marvel. The wonder.
Sweets even sweeter.
The spell all are under.

– – – – – – – – – – – – – – – –

Snow visits winter.
Spring watches it leave and melt
into happy tears

Snowman's Lament

Frosty was melting.
Fun-loving, no longer.
Miserable. Gloomy.
Sedentary somber.

Prayed for polar vortex.
Halt his harsh decline.
Arctic gusts, hail, icicles.
Hypothermically sublime.

Insulated with parka,
muffler and mittens.
Corncob pipe abandoned.
Carrot nose frostbitten.

Milk a little more winter
from Spring's cooler days.
Survival from the elements
and sun's furnace rays.

Alas, it means goodbye.
Senescence, sweet sorrow.
Only a puddle now remains.
His time, only borrowed.

Often, we try to delay
the unfortunate inevitable.
Eke out a few more days –
with suffering insensible.

There'll be other seasons.
Other children, other snows.
Imagination, magic hats –
another Frosty show.

Snow

Falls in flakes
stealthily, silently,
Bride white
innocence.

Flocks trees.
Blankets ground.
Wintery cloak
alabaster.

Sometimes a
welcome guest –
a visit for
just one day.

Or it remains.
A squatter.
Accumulating.
Imposing.

Lingers –
loses
part of its purity,
its virtue.

New coat
hides all sins.
Temporary
disguise.

Thaws. Refreezes.
Quiet
footsteps now
crackling and crunchy.

Until rain,
warm wind
persuade withdrawal –
exit in a splash.

Snow's arrival
embraced.
Departure –
a fond farewell.

March

Comes in like a lion.
Out like a lamb.

Wind and rain roar.
Simba's storms prowl
on unsuspecting prey.
Begins the chase
with tempest teeth
and rain claws,
forcing all quarry to
seek refuge, shelter.

Then, in the deluge,
a rainbow appears,
painting the sky
with hope and light.
Promise of protection.
Assurance the
torrent rage
only a temporary fear.

Daffodils silently signal
taming of the beast
with golden yellow trumpets.
Robins return in song
and make new nests.
Lamb, not lion,
withstands the weather –
with a romp and frolic to April.

March Madness

68 teams.
Neutral ground.
Fight to the finish
'til winner is crowned.

All with chance
to be number one.
Hope, eternal.
Place in the sun.

Will they play
top of their game
or let nerves
deny their acclaim?

Excitement. Drama.
Turmoil. Emotion.
Game plan succeeds
or fails from implosion.

Root for favorite,
underdog, longshot.
Those who survive
thicken the plot.

Orange ball.
red hoop.
Score a basket –
seconds to shoot.

Five wins in a row –
two teams remain.
Sixth, the championship.
Victory attained.

Crazed competition
comes to an end.
Madness now over 'till
March arrives again.

Daydreams

March – when begins
daydreams of spring.
Tulips, butterflies –
concertos birds sing.

Cherry blossoms.
Four leaf clovers.
Colorful gardens.
Jack rabbit jokester.

Nature walks. Waterfalls.
Old wooden bridge.
Fabled fairies flutter –
to stutter, sacrilege.

Kites in the sky
wish a day untethered.
Cotton ball clouds –
flying unfeathered.

Flower to flower,
petal bees pollinate.
Breeding new beauty
blooming creates.

Thunderstorm wakes
dreams of spring.
March has to happen.
Winter still clings.

April Fool-ishness

Got food poisoning!
Dingo ran away!
You're suspended!
Tornado's a comin'!
Bedbugs!
Moving to Mexico!
Lost my job!
Won the lottery!
See that Giraffe?!
Meteor! *Goodbye.*
Getting a helicopter!
IRS is here!
Those weren't chocolates!
Money's gone. *Hacked!*
It's Kale Salad Day!
Starting beekeeping!
Yes, a pony!
Out of toilet paper!
Hearing's gone. *What?*
Election fraud!
Put piranhas in the pond!
Caught five mice in *your* room!
Going to jail. Today!
Car got stolen!
Work for the C.I.A!
I'm older. *Much older!*
Not your father, *really!*
Lost my wallet!
Due in court!
Spiders. *Too many spiders!*
Computer caught fire!
Living two lives with lies!
Sister's in the hospital!
Banks closed – *for good!*
Someone stole your diary!
It's a worldwide pandemic!
(Sorry, it's no joke anymore)

Pollen Nations

Sugary-sweet nectar –
natural allure to attract
bees, beetles, butterflies,
bugs, birds and bats.

Pollen, stamen to stigma,
fertilized for reproduction.
Reciprocal relationships
allow both to function.

Shouldn't we help each other
in our own human way?
Enrich lives and benefit from
what's collected in our bouquet?

We need more pollination
for our breed to succeed.
Kindness and courtesy –
all should agree we need.

Flowers have no power
to sustain without support.
If we cannot do it together
our existence will fall short.

Nature provides the blueprint
for cooperation and compassion.
Let's make our own garden grow.
Turn apathy into action.

Smell the flowers, eat the fruit,
harbor our humanity.
It's not the bees I worry about,
but our own mortality.

Recognition of Rainbow

When colors bow
against the sky –
heart rich
with hope.

Red, the apex.
Crown of love.
Pinnacle passion.
Fortunate fortune.

Orange, second.
Gratitude of grace.
Appreciative awareness.
Thankful existence.

Yellow, next.
Light of life.
Gentle generosity.
Bountiful benevolence.

Green follows.
Germination of growth.
Hearten health.
Noble nature.

Then blue.
Wonder of water.
Placid peace.
Steadfast stability.

Indigo takes its turn.
Sanctity of spirit.
Augmented awareness.
Wakeful wisdom.

Bottom, violet.
Canton of creativity.
Encompassed empathy.
Salient selflessness.

No end to rainbow's gifts,
precious by any measure.
Riches of real wealth
shared by all who treasure.

Ladybug

Ladybug sits on basil leaf
smiling at caterpillar
dreaming about butterflies –
teasing that someday
it too will have wings.

They had been friends
long as each remember.
Basking in sunlit skies,
colorful pastels –
the garden they call home.

Small river meanders nearby –
nature's water fountain.
Mushrooms devour dampness,
grow among the daisies
nodding approval in the breeze.

Fireflies told ladybug
nothing lasts forever.
Robin's nest in tree abandoned
after little ones took flight.
Later, a basket for a child.

Clouds clutter the skyline.
Caterpillar cocoons.
Seeds fall, then grow anew.
Ladybug says hello to the sprouts.
Awaits her friend's wings.

As the Wind Blows

Something magical
about hot air balloons.
Nearly always rising
to the occasion.

Simple physics.
Hot air rises –
inside a balloon,
lifts it skyward.

An adventure
floating over rooftops
silently – except
for burner blasts.

Good pilot
can control the
ups and downs.
Wind, the unknown.

Where it goes,
no one knows.
Blows the balloon
anywhere it pleases.

On a balloon ride,
takeoff and landing
almost always assured –
destination uncertain.

Not unlike life –
where we all have
partial control over fate,
certainly not all.

Influences beyond control
also maneuver direction.
Shape our journey
with or without permission.

Whispering Woods

Go deeper into the forest
until you no longer hear
any sounds of civilization –
only heartbeat,
breath and
nature's symphony.

That's where
it whispers –
So quiet, you barely
catch the discourse.
Language never heard,
yet still understand.

You and the woods
begin a rapport
you didn't expect.
Fellowship. Communion.
Natural wisdom,
as its always been.

No longer hear
the roar of traffic,
sirens or airplanes –
A place of peace.
Tranquility. Calmness.
Abnormal focus.

Forest asks,
"Why not visit more often?"
You explain about all the things
modern society demands.
How it commands your time.
Stealing too many moments.

Then it whispers,
"Time is eternal. As I am.
Not caught up in the
spiral of civilization vortex.
Time is your time.
Spend it wisely."

Stop and Glow

Let illumination
inside you
radiate and
sparkle.
Speak less.
Glisten more.

Use honey
instead
of vinegar.
Thaw frigid
emotions
with warmth.

Be the spirit
that turns dark
into light.
Let moths
follow
your flame.

Tangle
snake's
forked tongue
with truth.
Soothe bruises
with soft cloth.

Visit your
intentions
regularly.
Smile your joy.
Smooth your edges.
Be exquisite.

Going to "L"

Laconic intent.
Loathe and lament.
Lady's lazy monogamy.
Lover larceny.
Legend in limbo.
Lips without libido.

Louver not loosened.
Lunar's dim lumen.
Lens without light –
Lasso not tight.
Leery lexicographer
Leaves limited luster.

Longitude lottery.
Leeward luxury.
Leak in lifeboat.
Linens soaked.
Locusts ravish.
Landslides lavish.

Pretzel Logic

Pleasure before business.
Every silver lining has a cloud.
If you're an egg, don't be a basket case.
Waste makes haste.
Every day has its dog.
Leap before you look.
If first you don't succeed, quit.
He who laughs last pays the check.
Fight fire with water.
Can't teach an old trick to a new dog.
Beauty isn't skin deep – skin is.
Impatience is a virtue.
If you don't make your bed, you can still lie in it.
Too many soups spoil the cook.
The early worm flips the bird.

Hiccup Help

Hold your breath.
Breathe into a paper bag.
Exhale while pinching nose
and mouth completely shut.
Pull on your tongue.

Sip ice water.
Drink from the
opposite side of the glass.
Suck on a lemon.
Eat a spoon of peanut butter.

Put a table knife
in glass of water
with blade flat
against forehead. Drink.
Give tongue a drop of vinegar.

Distract yourself
with a game or puzzle.
Do calculations in your head.
Tap skin on stern of neck.
Cotton swab back of throat.

Involuntary inhalation.
Diaphragm spasm.
Go away today!
Rhythm of ill measure.
Bout I could go without.

Pick your panacea –
remedy for relief.
Terminate the malady.
Note your antidote.
Counteract the grief.

It's just a hiccup,
just a hiccup,
just a hiccup
just a hiccup
after all.

Ugly Duckling

Nature waves her magic wand –
turns gosling into swan.
Sculptor takes ordinary stone –
carves it into artistry honed.

Caterpillar to butterfly.
Polliwogs to frogs.
Merciful metamorphosis
helps lift the florid fog.

Our duty, find beauty
in the darkest of days.
Storm clouds with silver linings.
Pathos patched with praise.

No mistakes, just lessons.
Displeasure to delight.
It may seem quite loathsome
but it doesn't make it right.

Ugly is what
humans do themselves.
Pollute a thriving river
in the name of wealth.

Kill another brother
whether war or decree.
Nothing is more sordid than
what we won't foresee.

There is no ugly duckling.
All a matter of perception.
Humans still have work to do.
We are, unfortunately, the exception.

Song to a Seagull

Clouds, camouflage –
hide in shadows,
shine in light.
Swoop over
calm blue waters,
turbulent indigo waves.

Flight travelogue
finds flock –
court and spark
itinerary for
new lovers as
wild things run fast.

Dog eat dog world –
competition
for sustenance.
Fisherman throw
catch guts to
fill bird bellies.

Sing your song,
earth and heaven,
to both sides, now.
Concert of busybodies
gossiping like
ladies of the canyon.

Roost on
ocean sand
and sea cliffs.
Moonlight
illumination as the
night rides home.

Recipe for Disaster

Begin with assault
and pepper spray.
Whip up upheaval.

Braise without praise.
Chop compliments.
Mince words.

A dash of danger
with a pinch of problems.
Place all in hot water.

Let suspicions simmer.
Marinate hate.
Cut to the bone.

Stew over spite.
Reconstitute resentment.
Render animosity.

Beat when boiling.
Whisk with a fist.
Caramelize lies.

Emulsify emotions.
Mix a roux.
Knead nightmares.

Dredge up prejudice.
Grease grievance.
Poach peace.

Aphrodisiac

Spanish fly.
Reason why?
Makes infatuation
into romance.

An erotic way
with feet of clay
to spice up a
lustful chance.

The one adored
gets very bored.
Persuade fondness
through a trance.

Need more than cupid,
don't be stupid.
Enamored passion
must be enhanced.

Sexy, turned on –
instantly drawn
to the lovey-dovey
lovesick advance.

Hot and heavy
in the silver Chevy.
Love potion
without the "can'ts."

A horny dream
or so it seems.
Heart waits for adoration
but never gets a glance.

Dunga Gin

Primal fermented grains
shutter and shatter
startled taste buds.
Train in locomotion.
Tiger in the tank.

Grants posh elegance
without the gauche.
Juniper fascinators
charm the derby nags,
normally shunting all.

Mint Juleps hold a grudge.
Grumble gaunt protests.
You're a better drink
to defy them,
Dunga Gin.

Not a Clue

Colonel Mustard
in the rural courtyard
pursuing petite poupon.

Mrs. Peacock
in the garden, weeding –
truly a phenomenon.

Mr. Boddy
in the tavern
drinking a draught.

Reverend Green
in the closet with
six squirrels and a bat.

Nurse White
in the nursery
taking a temperature.

Miss Scarlet, the harlot,
in a sitting room
far away in Worcestershire.

Yet, there was a murder.
As often the case –
few specific clues.

No revolver, rope,
dagger or candlestick.
Scissors turned the victim blue.

Suspects not where
they were supposed to be.
Devious or mischievous?

Successfully deduced they
could not be offenders
since no one was suspicious.

Lancelot

Lancelot used
his lance a lot.
Proved
his place in Camelot.

Fitting to the fable,
he strived to never fail.
Knight of roundtable.
Quest for Holy Grail.

Queen Guinevere,
his true heart.
Kept King Arthur
in the dark.

Alas, the affair exposed.
Guinevere, an abbess.
Lancelot disposed.
Hero to hermit oppressed.

Goodbye, fair maiden.
Goodbye, Lancelot.
Romance forsaken.
Goodbye, Camelot.

Nick's Knack

Despite his asthma
and awful cologne,
Nick had the talent
to resuscitate a
solemn audience
with subtle humor
kneaded into a
psychological dough
where witticism
reigned supreme.

The crowd would
attempt to wrangle
more minutes than
his set allowed,
earning him the wrath
of fellow comedians.
In receipt of such adulation,
it's an honest transgression
to forget the
conscience of his actions.

Any performer
following him
were silhouettes
in comparison.
You might say
Nick's knack
made patrons clap –
his shtick impact
held others back.
For that, his knack got flack.

Big Dipper

Took more than the rest.
Blatantly, boldly, with a little twirl.
Piled chip high, more than
three of us combined.
Perturbed. Bugged us.

Called him the *"Big Dipper."*
Boasted he could eat dip all day,
even with eyes closed. He could.
Except for the time we substituted
eel jelly while blindfolded.

Unharmed, his contorted face –
ugliest expression, ever.
Immediately called his BFF
to reveal what we had done.
We scattered like rabbits.

Big Dipper lost control.
Began dipping dip with a cup,
flaying it around the joint,
screaming, *"I'm no wet blanket!*
I can eat while wearing roller blades."

The allure of dip was more
than Big Dipper could bear.
Every get-together, every party –
no bowl of dip was safe.
"Meet me there!" he declared.

Taking more than his fair share,
engagements disappeared quickly.
Word got out about the obsession.
Invitations – thing of the past.
Big dip had no dip to dip.

Mayberry

Mayor Roy Stoner declared
May in Mayberry
a time of celebration.
May Day –
picnic in the park.
Music in the gazebo.
Dancing 'round the
maypole 'till dark.

Aunt Bee brought
sweet potato pie.
Helen made
persimmon salad
with mayo –
I don't know why.
Andy and Opie alike
brought their appetite.

It began to rain
to the townfolks' dismay.
Barney remarked,
"If we all had umbrellas,
maybe we could stay."
Otis smiled though the
mayhem and mishap –
soaked, a flask on his lap.

It was
Floyd the barber
who had the retort,
"Don't worry Pilgrims,
the showers will
bring Mayflowers."
Then asked Otis
for a little snort.

Episode featured
Willie Mays as a local
baseball wunderkind.
Guest of honor.
Autographs signed.
Black & white wingding
without commentary.
Another fine day in Mayberry.

Goodbye, Old Paint

Elephant's Breath
smells like hay.
Skimming Stone
tossed far away.

London Clay –
cobblestone bricks.
Pale Hound
rife with ticks.

Farrow's Cream
a soothing salve.
Tallow Mallow
was all they had.

Pelt crafted with
genuine Babouche.
Citron Blonde –
slurpy smooch.

Brood Mood –
Sulking Room Pink.
Calamine fine
with a little zinc.

Mahogany Morels.
Cooking Apple Green.
Rectory Red –
Incarnadine Queen.

Pigeon Parable.
Dove Tale.
Stone Blue Truth –
(actually, Quail.)

Such strange names
require explanation.
Paint chip pickers pulling from
their pigment of imagination.

Otis

Been with you
during all your
up and downs.

Rising to the very top.
Then – lowest
of the low.

Your cheerful bell
as you arrive –
all ready to go.

Quiet servant,
fulfilling
every command.

Calm even when
they really
push your buttons.

Those who fear you
take steps
to avoid you.

Your loyalty –
right on so
many levels.

Dependable.
Never once
going sideways.

You floor me –
but that's
another story.

The Other Side

Grass,
not always greener
on the other side.

Glass,
not always cleaner
on the other side.

Lass,
not always leaner
on the other side.

Splash,
not always deeper
on the other side.

Brash,
not always believers
on the other side.

Class,
not always keener
on the other side.

Task,
not always easier
on the other side.

Laughs,
not always keepers
on the other side.

Alas,
not always dreamers
on the other side.

John, Gone – 12/8/1980

On the evening news,
so many years ago –
the senseless murder
of John Lennon.

First of the Beatles to die.
Genius. Poet. Punster.
Rebel. Rabble-Rouser.
Hell of a musician.

It was all we talked about
at work the following day.
Made a mix tape of his best
to help a friend through the sorrow.

I know I cried, at least inside.
Like losing the smart aleck
older brother I never had.
Loss, heartfelt and heartsick.

His songs were a big part of
the soundtrack of our lives.
If I Fell. Norwegian Wood.
Nowhere Man. Ticket to Ride.

He was the Walrus. Day tripper.
Guiding us through uncertainty –
asking us to come together,
reminding that all we need is love.

He found out, unfortunately,
happiness really isn't a warm gun.
It was a hard day's night for us all.
Tomorrow never knows.

I think about the music he left behind –
his spirit, now across the universe.
Singing new songs of love, peace and harmony
in his favorite strawberry fields, forever.

Big John

First glance,
he was big.
And muscular.
Physically intimidating
with tattoos to match.

His wonderful ability
to laugh at himself
erased the fear.
Wore a grin that
invited you in.

Loved to sing
off key to music
while playing pickleball.
Occasionally, he cleverly
made up his own words.

John was loud.
Gentle.
Kind.
Caring.
Fun.

The courts are
way too quiet now.
I miss the singing.
The smiles.
The boisterous score announcements.

He found new friends
within our pickleball family.
Friends who now
endure the pain
of his absence.

I do hope
there is pickleball in heaven
and that he is patiently
waiting for all of us
to rejoin him in a game.

End Time

Difficult to think about
ones' end time.
Finality of it all.
People we leave behind.

When all good things
do come to an end –
will day of judgement
allow soul to ascend?

Privilege we call living
snuffed out like a candle.
Light of flame no longer –
expected or accidental.

Observe while it happens
to others, not our own.
Preparation for final days
by deaths bemoaned.

We learn to mourn.
Cherished spirits gone.
Memories not forgotten
and somehow live on.

When end time arrives –
Unwelcome thief.
Shanghai without apology.
Instigated grief.

Shine your life light
before the great unknown.
End time will come.
Time is but a loan.